Mennonite Education in a

POST-CHRISTIAN

World

Mennonite Education*in* *a*

POST-CHRISTIAN

World

Essays Presented *at the*
Consultation on Higher Education
Winnipeg, June 1997

Edited by Harry Huebner

CMBC Publications
Winnipeg, Manitoba
1998

CMBC Publications
600 Shaftesbury Blvd.
Winnipeg, Manitoba
R3P 0M4

Cover: Julie Fast

Canadian Cataloguing in Publication Data

Consultation on Higher Education (1997 : Winnipeg, Man.)

Mennonite education in a post-Christian world : essays presented at the Consultation on Higher Education in Winnipeg, June 1997

ISBN: 0-920718-59-0

1. Mennonite—Education, Higher—Congresses. 2. Mennonite universities and colleges—Congresses. I. Huebner, Harry, 1943– II. Title.

LC586.M4 C65 1997   371.07197   C98–920045–0

Printed in Canada by
Friesens
Altona, Manitoba
R0G 0B0

Table of Contents

Introduction

It has become difficult to document all the studies that inquire about the nature of the Christian college or university. There are simply too many. It is not clear precisely what drives this plethora of studies. Is it the march to secularization which has caught Christian colleges with the uncomfortable admission that they too have difficulties knowing how to do Christian education in the "post-Christian era?" Is it the critical questions that are being raised more and more sharply about the suppositions of liberalism in North America, requiring another look at how the charge of a biased education" is to be defended? Is it a new post-modern "permission" to be more intentionally Christian in our educational endeavours? Or perhaps it is rooted in more mundane forces like funding and low student enrollment.

Mennonite colleges are no exception to the current preoccupation with self-definition. Whether for precisely the same reasons may be less clear, but the last decade has seen significant shifts in Mennonite college education. In the United States there is renewed interest among Liberal Arts colleges in asking how they can more intentionally "educate for the church." At the same time several of these colleges recently have become universities. Whether these two forces are at odds with one another remains to be seen. In Winnipeg, the venue for the conference which resulted in this collection of essays, a federation of three existing Mennonite colleges is underway, which, if it comes to pass, will make it possible for students to receive, *inter alia*, a BA degree. This is a new venture for these colleges.

With changes like these comes the inevitable question: will the new be more or less faithful than the old? The challenge of Christian educators is to envision and embody institutions that will attract students, educate them, and thereby build the church and God's reign.

On June 13–15, 1997, a group of Mennonite College/Seminary/University staff, faculty, administrators and board members gathered to address these and related challenges. It had been five years since the last General Conference Higher Education Council event at Bluffton College (June 26–28, 1992) and two years since a similar event was held at Goshen College (March 23–26, 1995). Moreover, because 1997 was CMBC's 50th anniversary, former President John H. Neufeld issued the invitation for such an event to take place in Winnipeg. The agencies which sponsored this event were the General Conference

Higher Education Council, the Mennonite Church Board of Education, Associated Mennonite Biblical Seminary and Canadian Mennonite Bible College.

The planning committee consisted of representatives from each of the sponsors. The overall goal was to bring together the groups that make up the college community—staff, faculty, administrators and governors (we would have welcomed students, but this was summer and students are earning money during this time). It seemed worthwhile to have educators interact with one another on the question of what the Mennonite higher educational enterprise is all about.

We were especially pleased that Prof. Nancey Murphy, Fuller Theological Seminary, consented to be our keynote speaker. Gerald Gerbrandt, current President of CMBC, gave a presentation introducing us to the variety of institutions among us.

The rest of the conference was structured to focus on four components of institutional education—students, curriculum (visible and invisible), administration, and teaching. The papers in this volume are eleven of the twelve presented at the conference. The two presenters who characterize current students—Abe Bergen and Ritch Hochstetler—gave a joint presentation at the conference but their essays are printed separately in this volume.

Editorial efforts were kept to a minimum. The objective was to present the papers here as much as possible as they were delivered. Some stylistic adaptations and a few other minor changes were made. Readers should remember that these papers were prepared for oral delivery and not written presentation.

This publication was made possible with contributions from each of the sponsoring agencies. We thank them.

Harry Huebner
CMBC

1 A Theology of Education

Nancey Murphy[1]

Changes in Higher Education Gertrude Himmelfarb describes a series of revolutions in higher education during the twentieth century.[2] Until this century, she points out, most private colleges and universities were affiliated with a church. Gradually, however, almost all of them have either severed their denominational connections officially or else have maintained only nominal relations to a passive church.

It is generally thought that this "disestablishment" was a product of conflict between religion and science, provoked by Darwinism. Himmelfarb argues that the secularization actually has its roots in the Enlightenment and its philosophy of rationalism. "Indeed, it was the idea of 'culture'—a secular, rational, cosmopolitan liberal . . . culture—far more than . . . 'science' that lay behind the secularization of the university in the late-nineteenth and early-twentieth centuries" (16).

This disestablishment of the church Himmelfarb calls the first revolution in higher education. The second, she says, was the substitution of society for the church in the mission of higher education. After World War II, with the vast increase in the student population and the infusion of large sums of government money, the university acquired new functions, among them the solving of society's problems: poverty, pollution, and so on. In place of a *liberal* education, the university was now pleased to provide a *relevant* education, an education in what

---

[1]Associate Professor of Christian Philosophy, Fuller Theological Seminary.

[2]Gertrude Himmelfarb, "The Christian University: A Call to Counterrevolution," *First Things* (January 1996): 16-19.

society deemed to be useful or needful.

Having committed itself to solving society's problems, the university could hardly ignore the problems of its own students and so became a therapeutic institution, helping students to "find themselves." During the 1960s this therapeutic mission had as its corollary the empowerment of students, and thus the socially conscious university also became a highly politicized one.

"It was also inevitable," she says, "that a university eager to redress the ills of society would be called on to reflect the composition of society—its racial, ethnic, and sexual population" (17). It was not long before this idea of inclusiveness or representativeness was extended not just to the students, but to the very curriculum, requiring courses themselves to reflect the interests and identities of minorities.

Himmelfarb's main point is to identify a third revolution in academia, which she sees as much more significant than either the secularization or politicization. Today, she says, "many eminent professors in some of our most esteemed universities disparage the ideas of truth, knowledge, and objectivity as naive or disingenuous at best, as fraudulent and despotic at worst. Indeed, the very words—truth, knowledge, objectivity—now habitually appear in scholarly journals and books, in quotation marks, to show how spurious they are" (18). This "spirit of postmodernism," as she calls it, has become accepted almost unthinkingly by many professors and has put traditionalists on the defensive.

Himmelfarb wrote this piece for the installation last Fall of Baylor University's new president. She commended Baylor for being one of few institutions to resist the secularization (it intends to maintain a strong Baptist identity) and urged the institution to resist the third revolution as well.

I was well aware of the controversies at Baylor over what it means to be a Baptist university, having been caught in the crossfire while speaking there last Fall. So when I was asked to speak at this gathering, I was interested to know if the question in Mennonite higher education is whether to *be* Mennonite at all. My informants tell me that this is *not* the question. Rather, it is the more modest question of what difference being Mennonite makes to the theory and practice of higher education.

Mennonite higher education has so far bucked the trend toward secularization. I'm delighted, but I'm worried also. The intellectual and social pressures that compelled most of the denominational schools to make these changes are still very much in existence. Theological conservatism doesn't always prevent adaptation to cultural trends, as I've observed in my time with the Evangelicals at Fuller Seminary. It usually only means that the same adaptations will be made *later*.

So how are *you* going to resist the trend toward secularization, or at least toward nominal denominational identity? And how are you going to resist the third revolution—the rejection of the very idea of truth. Just say no?

In the time I have remaining I intend to do two things. First is to provide you with some philosophical and theological resources to back up that "no." Second is to share some related reflections on what Mennonite higher education might look like in the coming "postmodern" era.

Modernity One helpful resource for withstanding the pressures of Enlightened modernity is an understanding of the historical forces that produced the Enlightenment itself. Here I turn to a fascinating book by Stephen Toulmin titled *Cosmopolis*.[3] Toulmin contrasts the values of the Enlightenment with those of the Renaissance. After René Descartes, the ideal of human knowledge focused on the general, the universal, the timeless, the theoretical—in contrast to Renaissance valuing of the local, the particular, the timely, the practical. Why the change? Toulmin offers plausible speculations regarding the cultural climate that gave this new ideal its appeal. Descartes lived through the Thirty Years' War. The bloodshed and chaos that followed upon differences of belief lent urgency to the quest for *universal* agreement. If human reason was a faculty shared universally, then a new, secular culture founded on the deliverances of human reason must garner universal assent.

The result of this assumption about human reason was a view philosophers now call foundationalism. All disciplines must withstand the test of human reason. Theory of knowledge, epistemology, becomes first philosophy. Theology, ethics, even science, must now be provided with methodological prolegomena in order to show their credibility in the age of reason.

I claim that the entire history of the modern intellectual world could be recounted as the sad tale of a quest for universally recognizable foundations, and the failure, in one discipline after another, to find any such thing. There was the abortive attempt by some of the logical positivists to found science on sense data—the immediate deliverances of the senses. I have argued that a major cause of the split between liberals and conservatives in Protestantism was disagreement over the proper foundation for theology—scripture or religious experience.

---

[3]Stephen Toulmin, *Cosmopolis: The Hidden Agenda of Modernity* (New York: The Free Press, 1990).

Unfortunately, neither of these provides the requisite certitude. Alasdair MacIntyre and others argue that the major attempts to found morality on reason have all failed.

It is now clear to many that we are at some sort of turning point in intellectual history. Himmelfarb attributes the third revolution in academia to "the spirit of postmodernity." I believe, however, that much of what is called "postmodern" is actually nothing but a recognition of the failure to find indubitable foundations for universal knowledge. To turn to Nietzsche for the judgment that truth, knowledge, and objectivity are not only unattainable but *undesirable* is sour grapes. So I consider this so-called postmodernism to be essentially modern, in that it still assumes the modern ideal of knowledge—but with the bitter, further conclusion that such is not available.

In Toulmin's view, the truly *post*modern move might look more like a return to the values of the Renaissance: an appreciation for the timely, the local, the practical, and the particular.

Alasdair MacIntyre and the Way Ahead In my judgment, no philosopher has done more to lay out a way beyond the current crisis in academia than Alasdair MacIntyre. MacIntyre has worked in a number of areas in philosophy, but is currently best known for his work in philosophical ethics. In *After Virtue* he concluded that it is not possible to justify ethical claims apart from some *tradition* of moral reasoning.[4] That led him in two subsequent books to provide an answer to the question of how one could provide a rational justification for the acceptance of one such tradition over its rivals.[5]

MacIntyre's answer to this question is extremely important. Among thinkers who adequately recognize the problems of particularity and historical relativity, no one has provided a better account of how relativism can be avoided. I will not try to summarize his conclusions here. What is most important for our purposes is to explore his conception of tradition-dependent rationality, and to see that the recognition of a limited plurality of large-scale intellectual traditions need not result in relativism.

According to MacIntyre, traditions generally originate with an

---

[4]Alasdair McIntyre, *After Virtue,* 2d ed. (Notre Dame: University of Notre Dame Press, 1984).

[5]Alasdair MacIntyre, *Whose Justice? Which Rationality?* (Notre Dame: University of Notre Dame Press, 1988); and *Three Rival Versions of Moral Enquiry: Encyclopaedia, Genealogy, and Tradition* (Notre Dame: University of Notre Dame Press, 1989).

authority of some sort, usually a text or set of texts. The tradition develops by means of successive attempts to interpret and apply the texts in new contexts. Application is essential: traditions are socially embodied in the life stories of the individuals and communities who share them, in institutions, and in social practices.

In his recent book, *Three Rival Versions of Moral Enquiry*, MacIntyre distinguishes three major traditions in contemporary Western thought, which he labels Encyclopaedia, Genealogy, and Tradition. The first is named for its classic text, *The Encyclopaedia Britannica* (ninth edition), which enshrined the Enlightenment view of objective standards of rationality and universal morals. This tradition, he claims, has been effectively criticized by the Genealo-gists—Friedrich Nietzsche and his followers. As a current competitor to the Nietzschean view that all moralities need to be unmasked to reveal the interests behind them, MacIntyre offers his renewed version of the Aristotelian-Thomist tradition. Thus, MacIntyre sees two live options for the future of academia: Thomas or Nietzsche.

I, however, see three. I suggest that MacIntyre's account is typically Catholic, while the Genealogical tradition is in the line of descent from Augustine to the mainline Reformers. The fact that these two options can be associated with major theological positions suggests that we might find other possibilities by considering different *theological* positions.

In general, Catholic theologians have been more optimistic than Protestants regarding human capacities for knowledge. This optimism can be traced to the fact that Thomas developed an account of the hierarchical ordering of the capacities of the soul that was different from the account Protestants inherited from Augustine. For both Augustine and Thomas, the soul was conceived as hierarchically ordered, and the proper "chain of command" was from higher faculties to lower. For Augustine, the will was the highest function of the soul, above the intellect. Thus, when the will falls it corrupts all lower faculties, including the intellect; in Calvin's terms, the fall entails total depravity.

Thomas took the intellect to be the highest of human faculties. Since it is above the will the fall does not affect it directly. Humans can still fall into error, when the will leads them to form judgments prematurely, but the capacities for knowledge are not intrinsically darkened or depraved.

In MacIntyre's version of Thomist epistemology, he concentrates on the intellect *embodied in social practices*. A *social practice* is an important concept for MacIntyre for a variety of reasons. He defines it as follows:

> By a 'practice' I am going to mean any coherent and complex form of socially established cooperative human activity through which goods internal to that form of activity are realized in the course of trying to achieve those standards of excellence which are appropriate to, and partially definitive of, that form of activity, with the result that human powers to achieve excellence, and human conceptions of the ends and goods involved, are systematically extended.[6]

What is important for our purposes is the specification that social practices aim inherently at the realization of *goods* internal to those practices. Thus, MacIntyre's account of the socially embodied intellect is one in which the intellect itself aims intrinsically at a variety of goods. This is not to say that social practices, including those relating to the acquisition of knowledge, cannot be deformed or distorted (by corrupt institutions, or by the lack of appropriate virtues on the part of participants), but it is a more optimistic view of the nature of social practices than we find in the Genealogical tradition.

Nietzsche set out to show that the will-to-power conceals itself under the guise of the will-to-truth. If we redescribe Nietzsche's will-to-power in theological terms as wanting to be like God (cf. Gen. 3:5), his account is strikingly like what an Augustinian Christian would expect—apart from any concepts of grace, regeneration, or revelation.

Michel Foucault, an important interpreter of Nietzsche, has developed a view of knowledge parallel to MacIntyre's in many respects, and these very similarities make the difference at one point all the more striking. Both are thoroughly historicist in their understandings of epistemology; both employ a genealogical method; both regard knowledge as originating from social practices. But whereas MacIntyre takes such practices to lead to truth, Foucault concentrates on practices of social control, and aims to show how they distort human knowledge. For Foucault, there is an essential connection between knowledge and power, and it inevitably deludes us.

A Radical Reformation Alternative I now want to sketch some outlines of a radical reformation alternative to both Thomas and Nietzsche. I do believe that MacIntyre's account of the epistemological

---

[6]*After Virtue,* 187.

scene is the best available.[7] Yet his account has at least two major weaknesses. First is the overly optimistic evaluation of social practices and thus of the capacities of the (socially embodied) intellect. A second is that he has not been able (in his own estimation) to provide conclusive reasons to reject the Genealogical tradition. I claim that his epistemological account can be repaired, first, by *acknowledging* the (measure of) truth in the Genealogists' account of the epistemic distortions caused by the will to power, and, second, by providing a more nuanced account of social practices.

James McClendon has set out to produce a systematic theology in light of the radical-reformation heritage.[8] In his first volume, *Ethics,* he develops an account of social practices comparable to MacIntyre's. However, by invoking the biblical concept of *principalities and powers,* McClendon forges a concept of *powerful practices* that has neither the essential optimism of MacIntyre's account nor the essential pessimism of Foucault's account of the relations between power and knowledge.

The biblical concept of the powers has been lost to view in the course of Christian history, having been identified with the angels and demons of the medieval world view. The biblical concept of the powers developed from the concepts of the alien gods of Old Testament understanding. In the Near East, power was inevitably associated with gods, and gods were linked with politics and society.

"In the New Testament the powers retain their status subordinate to God, and also their political role: they are God's creatures (Col. 1:15-17), fallen and rebellious (Eph. 2:1ff; Gal. 4:1-11), and may be identical with empire and its lords (Rom. 13:1-4)" (174). The mission of Jesus is understood as conflict with and conquest of these powers. In the epistles this conflict is typically represented in summary form, as in Colossians 2:15 *REB*: "There he disarmed the cosmic powers and authorities and made a public spectacle of them, leading them as captives in his triumphal procession." In the Gospels, this conflict is portrayed in narrative form, and the opponents are no longer called the "principalities and powers," but are human overlords of state and

---

[7]See Nancey Murphy, *Anglo-American Postmodernity: Philosophical Perspectives on Science, Religion, and Ethics* (Boulder, CO: Westview Press, 1997), chap. 3.

[8]James Wm. McClendon, Jr., *Ethics: Systematic Theology, Volume I* (Nashville, TN: Abingdon Press, 1986); and *Doctrine: Systematic Theology, Volume II* (Nashville, TN: Abingdon Press, 1994).

temple, or demonic forces that sponsor illness and madness. McClendon says:

> Note further that the contra-power that Jesus . . . mounts against these is nothing less than the whole course of his obedient life, with its successive moments of proclamation, healing, instruction, the gathering of a redemptive community, and costly submission to the way of the cross and its death and resurrection (174).

Wherever Christ's victory is proclaimed, the corrupted reign of the powers is challenged, and yet they remain in being—in the time between the resurrection and the final coming of Christ, they remain in an ambiguous state. They delimit and define the social morality of Jesus' followers; to them the disciple must witness concerning the reversal of power achieved in Christ's resurrection. There is a hint in the New Testament that the final destiny of all these powers—civil, military, economic, traditional, cultural, social, *and religious*—will be not their abolition but their full restoration (Eph. 1:10; 3:10). "So the task of Christians confronting a world of *powerful practices* (as we may now call them) requires almost infinite adjustments, distinction, and gradations" (176).

Just as Jesus recognized the religion of his own day as among the powers, Christians today must recognize the power of institutionalized religion. Yet this need not deter them from the attempt to witness to the powers of the world by forming communities in which social structures and practices can more closely approximate God's will for the ordering of human life. Here is a powerful antidote to modern individualism: the church must be a new counter-society.

Now, my proposal is that we keep MacIntyre's account of tradition-based rationality, including his (and Foucault's) recognition of the role of social practices in the acquisition of knowledge. However, we need to use McClendon's account of powerful practices to correct both MacIntyre's and Foucault's views. That is, while the social practices of research and education can be corrupted, they need not be if only the will-to-power can be tamed.

I further suggest that a set of social practices characteristic of the radical reformation heritage provides just exactly the remedy needed to tame the will-to-power. The practice of nonviolence is the refusal to use physical force against another. What John Howard Yoder describes as "revolutionary subordination" is a strategy for righting injustices without the use of any power other than that of the imagination. The separation of church and state is the rejection of institutional longing for alliance with the power of the state. Finally, learning to live simply reduces the need for power to defend one's economic privileges.

In addition, radical-reformation churches have contributed to the development of what might be called a "Christian epistemic practice"—a communal practice aimed at the pursuit of truth. In general, this practice involves procedures and criteria for judging teaching, prophecy, and decisions as being or not being of the Spirit of Christ.[9]

Consistency with the Scriptures has served as the primary *criterion* for decision-making among the radicals. However, the *practical test* of consistency is the agreement of the entire community—whether the issue be the conduct of an individual in the local community, the distinctives of the radical movement as a whole, or a theological debate with outsiders. The *means* of reaching agreement is open discussion in the context of prayer. Note that this discernment is an instance of a social *practice* as defined by MacIntyre.

There is an important connection between discernment, as the radicals understood it, and the power-limiting practices described above. Pilgram Marpeck (1495?-1556) was committed to the *sola scriptura* principle, but without the aid of the Holy Spirit, he maintained, the Scriptures could not be interpreted or explained. The most subtle temptation besetting the Christian is to ascribe to the Holy Spirit what is actually one's own human opinion. "Ah, my brethren," he warns, "how diligently and carefully we have to take heed that we do not consider our own impulse the impulse of the Holy Spirit, our own course the course and walk of Christ."[10] We might say, how easy it is to be self-deceived about self-serving teachings, and how tempting it is to invoke the authority of the Holy Spirit to augment one's own power.

Consequently, Marpeck offered four signs by which to judge the impulses behind one's own or a fellow Christian's teaching:

First is love for God and to grant to my neighbor that which God has granted and given me for His praise and the salvation of my soul. Second is a devaluation and giving up of life unto death to suffer for the sake of Christ and the Gospel and all patience. Third, to realize when God unlocks or opens a door that one may enter the same with the teaching of the Gospel. No one shall open a door which God has not opened, in order that the office

---

[9]For a more detailed account of these practices, see Murphy, *Theology in the Age of Scientific Reasoning*, chap. 5.

[10]Torsten Bergsten, "Two Letters by Pilgram Marpeck," *Mennonite Quarterly Review* 32 (July 1958): 198.

of the Holy Spirit remain His own and free. For He it is who opens and no one closes, He closes and no one opens, in order that the pearls not be cast before swine. . . . Fourth, that one be free and sound in teaching and judgments and in truth, in order that none speak unless Christ work through his Holy Spirit . . . . These four parts are the true proof that the compulsion is of the Holy Spirit; also that it brings forth fruit at each season.[11]

The criterion of willingness to suffer and even to die is particularly interesting, for our purposes, in that it is a clear acknowledgement of the potential connection between theological teaching and self-interest. Consequently, teaching that is clearly in *disregard* of one's own survival has greater warrant to be accepted as authentic. The fourth criterion, the freedom of the teacher, arose from Marpeck's reaction to teaching distorted by the attempt to maintain church-state unity.

I suggest that what we see here is a social practice aimed at discerning truth, which adequately takes account of the distorting influences of the will-to-power and, in the happy case, counteracts it in a variety of ways: by listening to the least of the brethren (and sisters), by requiring unity, by deliberately favouring teaching that flies in the face of the will to survive. And all of this is taken to be a means of allowing the Holy Spirit (rather than self-interested individuals) to have the last word. While this practice was developed for practical decisions within the church, it is not irrelevant to scholarly enquiry, as its adaptation to the theological disputation demonstrates.

Note that the practices of nonviolence, simple living, and revolutionary subordination produce people with the *virtues* needed in order for the practice of discernment to succeed.

Consequences for Mennonite Higher Education I now want to try to pull together these various philosophical and theological strands in order to draw some concrete conclusions for the future of Mennonite higher education. My conclusions fall under three headings, but they are all interrelated: first, the legitimacy of tradition-based educational systems in general, and thus of Mennonite higher education that is thoroughly steeped in its own formative texts; second, the priority of moral formation to the intellectual life and the priority of theology to moral formation; and, third, an example of how a different theology leads, via a different form of life, to a different perception of reality—thus suggesting that a Mennonite theological and ethical perspective has implications for the entire curriculum.

---

[11]Ibid., 199.

First I will say a little about the legitimacy of tradition-based education. Recall the account I have pieced together from MacIntyre, Toulmin, and Himmelfarb: The Enlightenment began with the assumption that knowledge must provide a timeless and universal perspective. The goal was to get away from the conflicting authorities that emerged in the Reformation. But recent appreciation for cultural, rather than religious, diversity has led, first, to a smorgasbord approach to education, and most recently to a cynicism about any sort of truth.

I claimed that MacIntyre provides a third alternative: neither the demand for universal reason nor cynicism and relativism. Rather, what is called for now is the recognition that, as MacIntyre says, outside of all tradition one is morally and intellectually destitute. It is our traditions that give us the resources for justifying our actions as well as truth claims. Recognition of this tradition-dependence of rationality is not the same as limitless relativism, first, because there are not so many legitimate competitors within our culture and period of history; second, because it is possible for these traditions to compete meaningfully with one another, and occasionally it is possible to argue, in the public forum, that one tradition is rationally superior to its rivals.

MacIntyre has spelled out some of the consequences of his position for higher education in the last chapter of *Three Rival Versions*. He envisions that the wider society might be "confronted with the claims of rival universities, each advancing its own enquiries in its own terms and each securing the type of agreement necessary to ensure the progress and flourishing of its enquiries by its own set of exclusions and prohibitions, formal and informal" (234).

I have suggested that our own radical reformation tradition is indeed distinct in its point of view and form of life from the several traditions that MacIntyre recognizes: the outworn Enlightenment or Encyclopaedist tradition, the Nietzschean tradition, and MacIntyre's own Aristotelian-Thomist tradition. Furthermore, our tradition seems peculiarly well suited to address the current crisis in academia. With the Nietzscheans we can recognize the tendency of the will-to-power to obscure the truth, and in addition provide guidance for workable social and epistemic practices aimed at developing the capacity to live (and think and do research) without the assertion of power.

Thus it is entirely appropriate to continue to develop Mennonite institutions of higher education with distinctive practices and a distinctive perspective on reality. Such particularity is likely to contribute to the universal good.

The role of these power-renouncing practices, and of the virtues it takes to participate in them, leads directly to my second point: the priority of the ethical and theological to the rest of the intellectual life. The modern assumption has been that theoretical reason comes first and stands in judgment of both theology and ethics. Furthermore, right understanding precedes right action. The account I have been developing makes it clear that these orders of priority need to be reversed. Moral formation aimed at subduing the will-to-power is a necessary *prerequisite* for seeing reality aright. But how do we know that this is the case? I have hinted that such a recognition of the priority of the ethical to the intellectual requires *theological* grounding. For Nietzsche it was, perhaps, an Augustinian reading of (unregenerate) human nature. Many of us find more authentically biblical justification for the claim. The practical consequence is that we cannot expect right living to follow a good education: moral formation in seminaries and colleges must be a first priority.

I cannot adequately argue here for the priority of the theological to ethics, and of ethical formation to the intellectual life. I turn instead to an illustration of how radical reformation theology and ethics can impact one's understanding of biological evolution. This is in order to suggest that parts of the curriculum even as far-removed from theology as the natural sciences may be affected by our theological standpoint.

I have long been intrigued by a passage at the end of Emil Brunner's *Revelation and Reason:*

> Man as sinner is like a usurper who has illegally wrenched a city out of the hands of the king and brought it under his own authority, which is really a false sovereignty. Thus man as sinner, in his imagined and false autonomy, has brought life under the dominion of the reason severed from God and the arbitrary sway of instinct. All human powers stand in an order that is disorder. Life in the city goes on [in] its ordered way, it is true; much goes on as though it were not the usurper but the rightful lord who is in power. The more impersonal the sphere, the less disturbance there is; the more personal, the greater disturbance. Mathematical thought and technical dexterity are far less affected than marriage and the life of the family. The disturbance is great wherever personal human relations are involved; the disorder itself, however, is the usurpation as such, that is, the negative relation to God. Now the meaning of the Christian revelation is this: that by it, where it is received in faith, the rightful King is reinstated in the seat of authority. This means that everything in the city becomes different; but everything is not altered to the same degree. Through Christ we do not receive a different mathematics, physics, or chemistry, but we do find a

different kind of marriage, family life, a different kind of public justice.[12]

Notice that Brunner does not mention biology. I want to take an example from my own recent work, from chapter 5 of *Reconciling Theology and Science: A Radical Reformation Perspective,* in which I suggest a relationship between evolutionary theories in biology and our radical reformation theology and ethics.[13]

One of the reasons that Christians of all sorts have objected to Darwin's evolutionary theory is that it has led to social Darwinism, that is, to the moral commendation of competition and survival of the fittest in the social and economic spheres. Some historians, however, have called into question the temporal priority of Darwin's thesis, suggesting instead that Darwin perceived and emphasized competition over cooperation because of his conditioning by the competitive economic theories of his day.

A more recent controversy concerning the relation between ethics and evolution involves sociobiology. Sociobiologists claim to provide a naturalistic account of human morality, explaining altruism, for instance, as the product of natural selection. That is, some suggest that because altruistic actions are most often beneficial for family members, who share many of the same genes, altruism therefore increases the chance of survival *for one's genes.* The development of the trait is thereby explained by natural selection.

What strikes me about this argument is how un-Christian is the ethic it is taken to explain. Or, to put it the other way around, if this is the "ethic" of the biological world, then Christian morality is profoundly anti-biological. We Christians are not enjoined to sacrifice most for those who are biologically closest to us. Quite the contrary! Jesus' teachings are shockingly anti-family. Instead, the Christian's first loyalty must be the new family of God, which is one new "race," made out of both Jews and Gentiles. If anyone is to be singled out for special care it is the "other": the stranger, the enemy.

So it is clear that there are a variety of ways of relating evolutionary biology and ethics. But what is the content of the ethic? And does ethics follow from biology or is it the other way around? There are theological connections as well. That is, if God is creator of the whole world, then

---

[12]Emil Brunner, *Revelation and Reason* (Philadelphia: Westminster Press, 1947), 429.

[13]Nancey Murphy, *Reconciling Theology and Science: A Radical Reformation Perspective* (Kitchener, ON: Pandora Press, 1997).

we ought to look for signs of God's character and of God's will for our lives in the natural world, as well as in Scripture. When biologists emphasize a picture of nature as a scene of competition for survival—of nature "red in tooth and claw"—how are we to reconcile this with a picture of a self-sacrificing God who reaches out to save the weak, the lost, and even the enemy?

What is needed is a change of perspective. Holmes Rolston reconciles the "morality" of evolutionary biology with a Christian ethic of self-sacrifice, as well as with the self-sacrificial character of God, by teaching us to see the work of God not in the predator but in the prey. I quote his beautiful prose at length.

> The Earth is a divine creation and scene of providence. The whole natural history is somehow contained in God, God's doing, and that includes even suffering, which, if it is difficult to say simply that it is immediately from God, is not ultimately outside of God's plan and redemptive control. God absorbs suffering and transforms it into goodness. . . .
>
> [N]ature is . . . cruciform. The world is not a paradise of hedonistic ease, but a theater where life is learned and earned by labor, a drama where even the evils drive us to make sense of things. Life is advanced not only by thought and action, but by suffering, not only by logic but by pathos. . . .
>
> This pathetic element in nature is seen in faith to be at the deepest logical level the pathos in God. God is not in a simple way the Benevolent Architect, but is rather the Suffering Redeemer. The whole of the earthen metabolism needs to be understood as having this character. The God met in physics as the divine wellspring from which matter-energy bubbles up . . . is in biology the suffering and resurrecting power that redeems life out of chaos. . . .
>
> The secret of life is seen now to lie not so much in the heredity molecules, not so much in natural selection and the survival of the fittest, not so much in life's informational, cybernetic learning. The secret of life is that it is a passion play. Things perish in tragedy. The religions knew that full well, before biology arose to reconfirm it. But things perish with a passing over in which the sacrificed individual also flows in the river of life. Each of the suffering creatures is delivered over as an innocent sacrificed to preserve a line, a blood sacrifice perishing that others may live. We have a kind of "slaughter of the innocents," a nonmoral, naturalistic harbinger of the slaughter of the innocents at the birth of the Christ, all perhaps vignettes hinting of the innocent lamb slain from the foundation of the world. They share the labor of the divinity. In their lives, beautiful, tragic, and perpetually incomplete, they speak for God; they prophesy as they participate in the divine pathos. All have "borne our griefs and carried our sorrows."
>
> The abundant life that Jesus exemplifies and offers to his disciples is that of a sacrificial suffering through to something higher. There is something divine about the power to suffer through to something higher. The Spirit of

God is the genius that makes alive, that redeems life from its evils. The cruciform creation is, in the end, deiform, godly, just because of this element of struggle, not in spite of it. There is a great divine "yes" hidden behind and within every "no" of crushing nature. God, who is the lure toward rationality and sentience in the upcurrents of the biological pyramid, is also the compassionate lure in, with, and under all purchasing of life at the cost of sacrifice. God rescues from suffering, but the Judeo-Christian faith never teaches that God eschews suffering in the achievement of the divine purposes. To the contrary, seen in the paradigm of the cross, God too suffers, not less than his creatures, in order to gain for his creatures a more abundant life.[14]

This interpretation of suffering is consistent with Anabaptist thought, in which the suffering of Christians is not generally seen as a punishment for sins, but rather as redemptive participation with Christ in the expected consequences of obedience to God in the midst of a sinful world. Hans Hut proclaimed "the Gospel of Christ crucified, how He suffered for our sake and was obedient to the Father even unto death. In the same way we should walk after Christ, suffering for his sake all that is laid upon us, even unto death."[15]

It is interesting to note that several of the original Anabaptist writers extended this account of human suffering to include "the Gospel of All Creatures." Hut taught that the suffering of animals and the destruction of other living things conforms to the pattern of redemption through suffering, and in its own way preaches the Gospel of Christ Crucified.[16] The parallels with the writings of Holmes Rolston are striking.

So I am suggesting that a different theological perspective, along with a different moral formation, can predispose us to see reality differently than do those in other traditions. In this particular case, a radical reformation perspective leads to a hermeneutic of suspicion directed toward the standard histories of science, to the ability to see structures of economic power as potential sources of distortion in Darwin's perception of nature.

Yet I want to emphasize that this is not merely negative or critical. In fact, biologists are now recognizing that the competitive account of

---

[14]*Zygon: Journal of Religion and Science* 29, no. 2 (1994): 205-229; quotation 218-220, *passim.*

[15]Rollin Armour, *Anabaptist Baptism* (Scottdale, PA: Herald Press, 1966), 78, quoting Hans Hut, *Vom Geheimnus der Tauff.*

[16]Armour, *Anabaptist Baptism,* 82.

evolutionary processes has been overstated. Much more attention needs to be paid to the role of cooperation, both within and among species.

Conclusion   It's time to sum up. I began with an account of the modern secularization of institutions of higher education, and of late-modern cynicism regarding knowledge and truth. I argued that Alasdair MacIntyre's recognition of the tradition-dependent character of all enquiry provides a way ahead for academia in general and in particular offers a rationale for the particularity of Mennonite higher education.

I suggested that our radical reformation emphasis on power-renouncing practices provides resources for an account of the possibilities of human knowing that responds to a widespread recognition of the distorting influence of the will-to-power. In addition, from the perspective of those who have learned to live in the world without power—from the perspective of the prey rather than the predator, from the perspective of those living in solidarity with the weak and the outcast—reality in all its aspects looks somewhat different. This perspective needs to be reflected all across the curriculum.

I add one final note. The moral formation of students (and of ourselves as well) has to be an ongoing process. We are not speaking only of information to be imparted, but of a specific form of life to be adopted and practiced in all aspects of campus life—it is as much a task for administrators, dormitory supervisors, and cafeteria workers as it is for professors and students. May God bless all of us in our attempts to become enough like Jesus to see the world aright.

----

2 Who Are We? Mennonite Higher Education[1]

Gerald Gerbrandt[2]

Introduction Reviewing present Mennonite efforts in higher education has been a fascinating and illuminating experience, especially when I consider it from the perspective of my own personal background. I grew up in southern Manitoba, the descendent of Mennonites who came to North America in the 1870s. At least to some extent they came in order to escape the encroachment of the larger world upon their secluded colonies in Ukraine. In southern Manitoba these simple but dedicated Mennonites developed their own schools, but schools remained on a fairly elementary level. In the 1920s many of these Mennonites chose to flee to Mexico rather than participate in provincially administered public schools. When my father completed grade 8 he wanted to continue his studies in high school, but in his community considerable opposition to such higher education remained. In the early 1960s some of my friends in the Altona high school were the first in their family to be allowed to attend high school. The Low German saying, *je jelieda, je fechieda* (roughly translated: the more educated, the more perverted) was close to the hearts of many Mennonites in the southern Manitoba world of my youth.

The attitude of my particular slice of the North American Mennonite people, may have been extreme in its suspicion of education, but I do not believe it was unique, or perhaps even that atypical. Just consider

---

[1]In preparing this presentation I wrote a letter to each of the schools listed asking for information and help. I am gratified by the very positive response. I received personal responses, catalogues, financial statements, policy manuals, and even histories of some of the schools, and more. Without such generous help this paper would not have been possible. I trust I have not misrepresented the schools too badly in what I say about them.

[2]President, Canadian Mennonite Bible College, Winnipeg, Manitoba.

the Amish and Hutterite wings of the larger Mennonite family. I have the impression that even among those Mennonite groups which tended to be more positive about education there were those with significant questions about higher education, or post-secondary Mennonite schools which offered programs other than biblical studies or vocational preparation. In some communities these questions led to downright mistrust of all educators.

I was fascinated by my review of present Mennonite efforts in higher education, to some extent at least, because nowhere was there any evidence of such a history or background. The reports from the schools emphasized growth, expansion of facilities, greater involvement in accreditation and cooperation with universities and government. Given the tremendous energy and resources we Mennonites give to the task of higher education, it is amazingly far removed from the *je jelieda, je fechieda* approach of many of our ancestors. Hesitancy to cooperate with the government in education has been replaced by aggressive negotiations with government for recognition and financial support. We have come a long way, or so it appears.

My task today is to introduce you to Mennonite higher education. I will do this in four parts. First, I will introduce the schools themselves, in the process organizing them into various categories or groups. Second, I will suggest some characteristics of the present Mennonite effort in higher education. Third, I will draw attention to some differences between the Canadian and America schools. And last, I will make some observations or raise some questions about Mennonite higher education.

Before beginning such a description, however, one must determine which schools to include in the category of "Mennonite Higher Education." At least two questions must be answered in this process— "What is Mennonite?" and, "What type of relationship is a school required to have to the Mennonite people or church in order to be considered a Mennonite school?" Determining what is Mennonite is more complex than at first may appear. Harold S. Bender, for example, includes Christian Missionary Alliance schools in his listing of Mennonite Bible schools in the *Mennonite Encyclopedia*.[3] Should schools of the Brethren in Christ, a church body which works with Mennonites in Mennonite Central Committee be included? For this presentation I have understood the term Mennonite more narrowly as

---

[3]H. S. Bender, "Bible Schools," *Mennonite Encyclopedia* (Scottdale, PA: Mennonite Publishing House, 1969).

only including those church bodies which use the term "Mennonite" in their self-designation. One of the consequences of this is that Messiah College, a college of the Brethren in Christ, a college which is listed in the *Mennonite Yearbook* as belonging to the Council of Mennonite Colleges,[4] is excluded.

With one exception[5] I have expected schools to have a formal or structural relationship to a Mennonite church body. This excludes schools like Grace Bible Institute and the Mennonite School of Nursing in Normal, Illinois, both schools with strong historical ties to the Mennonite community, but at present with no formal relationship to a Mennonite conference. It also excludes schools like Providence College in Otterbourne, Manitoba, and Briercrest College in rural southern Saskatchewan, both schools with a significant portion of the student body coming from Mennonite congregations.[6] These criteria yield 23 institutions of Mennonite higher education in Canada and the United States.[7]

Introducing the Mennonite Schools of Higher Education

I will introduce the schools through four lists or tables.

Arranged in Order of Origin*

Bethel College – 1887
Goshen College – 1894 (Elkhart Institute of Science, Industry & the Arts)
Bluffton College – 1899 (Central Mennonite College)
Tabor College – 1908
Hesston College – 1909
Eastern Mennonite University – 1917 (Eastern Mennonite School)

---

[4]*Mennonite Yearbook 1996* (Scottdale, PA: Mennonite Publishing House, 1996), 150.

[5]The exception is Menno Simons College in Winnipeg, Manitoba. Menno Simons College is owned and operated by a society called "The Friends of Menno Simons College." I have included it both because of its obvious effort to be identified as Mennonite, as reflected in the name, and because it has invited the larger Mennonite conferences of Canada to participate in its governance.

[6]The portion of the student body at Providence is so high that recently the Chancellor of Providence College identified the school in a formal presentation to the government of Manitoba as related to the Mennonite community.

[7]Although Eastern Mennonite Seminary is governed as part of Eastern Mennonite University, to "hide" it within the larger university in this presentation seemed to me not to give it the recognition it should have. I thus have treated it as a separate entity, recognizing that formally this is not accurate.

Winkler Bible Institute – 1925
Bethany Bible Institute – 1927
Steinbach Bible College – 1936 (Steinbach Bible Institute)
Columbia Bible Institute (Mennonite Brethren Bible Institute/Bethel Bible
    Institute – 1936/1939)
Concord College (Mennonite Brethren Bible College) – 1944
Fresno Pacific University – 1944 (Pacific Bible Institute)
Associated   Mennonite   Biblical   Seminary   (Mennonite   Biblical
Seminary/Goshen Biblical Seminary) – 1945/1946
Canadian Mennonite Bible College – 1947
Eastern Mennonite Seminary – 1948
Rosedale Bible Institute – 1952 (Conservative Mennonite Bible School in
    Berlin, Ohio)
Mennonite Brethren Biblical Seminary – 1955
Conrad Grebel College – 1964
Aylmer Bible Institute – 1976
Institut Biblique Laval – 1976
Sharon Mennonite Bible Institute – 1977
Menno Simons College – 1989
Toronto Mennonite Theological Centre – 1990

*The dates given for the schools are not arbitrary, but there is considerable flexibility in designating a particular year as the year of origin for a school. Bethel College, for example, conceivably could have used 1877, the year a group meeting in Alexanderwohl decided to establish a Zentralschule, or 1882, the year H. H. Ewert first offered classes in Alexanderwohl on behalf of the school committee of the Kansas Mennonite Conference, or 1883, the year classes were initiated by the Halstead College Association, or 1887, the year the State of Kansas issued a charter to Bethel College, or 1893, the year Bethel College opened in Newton.

Arranged by Church Relationship
Mennonite Brethren
    Bethany Bible Institute
    Concord College
    Fresno Pacific College
    Institut Biblique Laval
    Mennonite Brethren Biblical Seminary
    Tabor College
    Winkler Bible Institute
Mennonite Church
    Eastern Mennonite University
    Eastern Mennonite Seminary
    Goshen College
    Hesston College
    Rosedale Bible Institute – Conservative Mennonite Conference

Sharon Mennonite Bible Institute (Association)
General Conference Mennonite Church
    Bethel College
    Bluffton College
Mennonite Church/General Conference
    Associated Mennonite Biblical Seminary
    Canadian Mennonite Bible College – Conference of Mennonites
      in Canada
    Conrad Grebel College – Mennonite Conference of Eastern
      Canada
Evangelical Mennonite Mission Conference
    Aylmer Bible Institute
Inter-Mennonite
    Columbia Bible College – Mennonite Brethren, General Conference
    Menno Simons College – no structural relationship to a church body, but
      Friends of MSC come from a number of Mennonite conferences
    Steinbach Bible College – Chortitzer Mennonite Conference, Evangelical
      Mennonite Conference, Evangelical Mennonite Mission Conference
      (Manitoba Conference)
    Toronto Mennonite Theological Centre – supported by conferences and
      schools representing the Mennonite Church, the General Conference,
      and the Mennonite Brethren

Arranged by Type of Institution

Seminary or Graduate
    Associated Mennonite Biblical Seminary
    Eastern Mennonite Seminary
    Mennonite Brethren Biblical Seminary
    Toronto Mennonite Theological Centre
Liberal Arts College
    "Traditional"
      Bethel College
      *Bluffton College
      *Eastern Mennonite University
      *Fresno Pacific University
      Goshen College
      Hesston College (junior college)
      Tabor College
    "Variations of the Traditional"
      Concord College
      Conrad Grebel College
      Menno Simons College
Bible College/Bible Institute
    Aylmer Bible School
    Bethany Bible Institute
    Canadian Mennonite Bible College

Columbia Bible College
Institut Biblique Laval
Rosedale Bible Institute
Sharon Mennonite Bible Institute
Steinbach Bible College
Winkler Bible Institute
*liberal arts colleges with graduate programs

Arranged in Country of Location

Canada	*United States*
Aymer Bible Institute	Associated Mennonite Biblical Seminary
Bethany Bible Institute	Bethel College
Canadian Mennonite Bible College	Bluffton College
Columbia Bible Institute	Eastern Mennonite University
Concord College	Eastern Mennonite Seminary
Conrad Grebel College	Fresno Pacific College
Institut Biblique Laval	Goshen College
Menno Simons College	Hesston College
Steinbach Bible College	Mennonite Brethren Biblical Seminary
Toronto Mennonite Theological Centre	Rosedale Bible Institute
Winkler Bible Institute	Sharon Mennonite Bible Institute
	Tabor College

Characteristics of the Present Mennonite Venture in Higher Education
I present the following four characteristics of our current Mennonite venture.

Mennonite higher education is an enormous enterprise.[8] Here I will consider two aspects: people and finances..

1) People. Over the years I have visited virtually all the schools listed so I knew that Mennonite higher education was a major enterprise, but

---

[8] I found the task of obtaining parallel and accurate statistics for each institution virtually impossible. Different schools have different fiscal years, different methods of calculating full-time equivalency, and different ways of classifying faculty and staff. The statistics I cite are all based on one full year. In most cases this is the 1996-1997 school year. A few schools do not use the academic year as the fiscal year. In those cases the 1996 fiscal year was used in finances. In one or two cases the 1996-1997 statistics were unavailable so I had to use the 1995-1996 numbers. I recognize that these differences preclude fine comparisons of the numbers. I believe they are accurate enough, however, to contribute to an overall picture of the Mennonite higher educational enterprise, and to do some comparisons among schools. If somehow an institution feels misrepresented, I apologize.

I was quite taken aback when I actually looked at the numbers. Mennonite higher education involves a huge number of people. Here are just a few statistics from our Mennonite schools:

a. *Total number of board members*: 361

b. *Total number of employees*: 1,759

c. *Total number of teaching faculty* (minimum 50% appointment): 559 (A further 250-300 serve as sessional instructors)

d. *Total number of students*: just under 12,000 (excluding the approximately 12,000 involved in Fresno Pacific's professional studies programs)

e. *Student full-time equivalent*: approximately 7,000

Largest institutions:

- based on number of students contacted: Fresno Pacific University

- based on number of students officially registered: Conrad Grebel College (ca. 2,800)

- based on student full-time equivalent: Eastern Mennonite University (ca. 1,074, plus Seminary. Bluffton, Goshen and Fresno are not far behind.)

Smallest institutions:

- Toronto Mennonite Theological Centre (15 students registered)

- Aylmer Bible Bible Institute, Institut Biblique Laval and Winkler Bible Instititue all registered between 30 and 45 students

2) Finances. Perhaps the single most impressive financial statistic is that in the last fiscal year the combined operating budgets of our Mennonite post-secondary institutions was just over $153,000,000.[9] Capital development projects were above this.

Of this $153,000,000 students pay approximately $100,000,000, or two-thirds, through tuition, rent, board, and auxiliary fees. Within the seminaries the students pay the lowest portion, approximately 25-30% of the total costs. Among Canadian schools there is a large range, with students paying as little as 20% and as much as 63% of all costs. The large range may be a little misleading, however, in that since some of these schools have such small student numbers that a drop in enrolment can very quickly have a major impact on the portion of the total budget covered by student fees. The much lower tuition fees in Canada

---

[9]All numbers are in Canadian dollars. In 1996-1997 a conversion of approximately 1:1.35 would produce the equivalent amount in US dollars.

compared to US schools does mean, however, that students generally do pay a much lower portion of all costs.[10] The US liberal arts colleges tend to expect student fees to produce approximately three quarters of the annual budget. Even if the much more significant financial assistance programs of the US colleges is taken into consideration, the difference remains substantial.

The second largest financial contributor to Mennonite higher education is the charitable donor. More than $24,000,000 was donated to these schools during the past year. This includes donations to the annual operating fund, as well as income from endowments on the assumption that at some point these endowments also came from donations. It does not include new endowment money or money donated for capital projects. Of this $24,000,000 approximately $6,000,000 came directly from the supporting church bodies, either through the larger conferences or directly from local congregations, with the remainder coming from private donors. Not surprisingly, donation support was highest for seminaries, second highest for Bible colleges/Bible institutes, and lowest for liberal arts colleges. This continuum was even more striking when only dollars coming directly from the church bodies were considered.

The government is also a significant partner in the Mennonite venture in higher education. US liberal arts colleges have tended not to receive major direct grants from the government (although this appears to be changing at least somewhat), but their financial assistance programs have been heavily subsidized by government grants. In Canada the lines between church and state have been drawn differently, with the result that the various levels of government have been more open to contributing to church schools, and the church has been more open to receiving government support.[11] Conrad Grebel College, for

---

[10]The discrepancy between Canadian and US tuition fees remains immense. Compare the full year tuition fees for the 1997-1998 academic year of the following three representative Canadian schools with three US colleges (all in Canadian currency):

Conrad Grebel/U of Waterloo:	$3,756	Eastern Mennonite:	$16,200
CMBC:	$3,000	Goshen:	$15,457
Columbia Bible College	$3,880	Fresno Pacific:	$15,187

[11]This may be even more obvious on the secondary level where Mennonite high schools in British Columbia, Saskatchewan and Manitoba all receive significant government funding. In Manitoba, for example, funding of private elementary and secondary schools is pegged at 50% of funding for public schools.

example, received more than $800,000 from the Ontario government, an amount which represented approximately 30% of its budget.[12]

Mennonite higher education remains very Mennonite. It is widely recognized that over the years church-related colleges tend to become more distant from the church body which founded them.[13] It is debated whether this is because the college is pushed away by the church, or because the college frees itself from the ties of the church, but the basic pattern seems clear. Merrimon Cuninggim examines this common development in his recent book, *Uneasy Partners: The College and the Church.*[14] He suggests three natural stages in the relationship between church and college. *First*, there is the period in which the church is the senior partner in the relationship, completely in control of the school. During this stage the colleges seldom question the church's sovereignty over them. This was the norm in most church colleges around the turn of the century when nearly 1,000 such colleges dotted the US landscape. The *second* stage period is one in which the church and college are roughly at even strength, a common pattern between 1930 and 1960. Gradually the *third* stage takes over in which the college moves into the primary position. Now the churches play the junior role. Church conferences and leaders may feel uncomfortable about, or even challenge their secondary status, but Cuninggim considers this a sign of maturity in the colleges. He suggests this is the norm today for most colleges except those related to the "'ultraconservative' Christian College Coalition." He speaks of those colleges which allow the

---

[12]At the time this paper was presented in June 1997, it was reported that CMBC, Concord College and Menno Simons College were negotiating with each other and the government of Manitoba regarding the possible development of a Mennonite College Federation. Since then the government and these three colleges have signed a Memorandum of Understanding in which the government commits itself to provide a $2,600,000 annual operating budget grant to the federation for at least three years, assuming the three colleges agree on satisfactory arrangements among themselves and the three bodies which own these colleges accept the details of the arrangements.

[13]Many books and articles could be cited which make this point. Note especially George M. Marsden and Bradley J. Longfields (eds.), *The Secularization of the Academy* (New York: Oxford University Press, 1992) and George Marsden, *The Soul of the American University: From Protestant Establishment to Established Nonbelief* (New York: Oxford University Press, 1994).

[14](Nashville, TN: Abingdon Press, 1994).

churches to "call their tune" as "outside the collegiate mainstream."[15]

Even a fairly quick study of Mennonite higher education makes it clear that our schools have remained very Mennonite. Presumably Cuninggim would suggest they have not yet entered the "mainstream." Cuninggim points out nine "alleged qualifications" frequently used to evaluate the church-relatedness of a college. He speaks somewhat sarcastically of admiring and demanding church folks who are happy, especially at ceremonial occasions, when these are met, and who are unhappy when the colleges are unable, or unwilling, to meet them. Although Cuninggim considers them inappropriate, and although they do have their real weaknesses, it is striking how Mennonite our schools are when they are evaluated by the qualifications listed by him.

1) Founding and historic associations. All 23 of the schools included were started within Mennonite communities, many directly by a Mennonite church body.

2) Structure and governance. The Mennonite origin of the schools continues in present relationships. The majority of the schools are formally owned by some branch of the Mennonite church, either by the North American denomination or by some regional or area conference. Virtually all of the schools not directly operated by Mennonite conferences have strong formal ties to some part of the Mennonite church body.[16] Of the 361 board members who govern the 23 Mennonite schools, 361, or approximately 94%, are members of the Mennonite church. Perhaps the one school with no official tie to any arm of the Mennonite church is Menno Simons College, and yet all 15 of its board members are Mennonite. I believe it is fair to say that all 23 schools are owned by the Mennonite church, many formally and legally, others indirectly, emotionally and practically.

3) Support—especially financial. Although the portion of the schools' operating budgets derived directly from church subsidy is small (4%), it does represent a very significant contribution—nearly $6

---

[15]Ibid, 38.

[16]For example, Bethel and Bluffton are not directly operated by the General Conference or one of its area conferences. And yet the Western District Conference of the General Conference elects members to the Bethel board, and both the Central District and the Eastern District elect members to the Bluffton board.

million annually.[17] Not surprisingly, seminaries were heavily supported by the church. Further, all schools reported that the vast majority of individual and corporate donations (a further 12%, or more than $18 million annually) came from members of the Mennonite church. All in all, Mennonite schools are very well supported by the Mennonite church.

4) Credentials of the college leaders. Of the 559 faculty teaching at Mennonite post-secondary schools, 428, or 77%, were reported to be members of the Mennonite church.[18] I believe the presidents of all schools except one are Mennonite.[19]

5) Students. At least four of the Mennonite schools have adopted a mission in which witness and service to those outside of the Mennonite community play an important role: Conrad Grebel, Menno Simons, Bluffton, and Fresno Pacific. In each case the portion of the total student body which is Mennonite thus is quite small.[20] On the other side, of the 23 schools 14 have student bodies which are more than 50% Mennonite. Hesston, in fact, increased its Mennonite percentage in the past few years. Nevertheless it probably is not coincidental that the schools with the lowest percentage of Mennonite students are also the ones which have experienced the most growth in the past few years.[21]

The last four qualifications used to measure church relatedness of a college are more difficult to quantify so I have simply listed them: course of study, campus life, religious affairs and provisions, and ethos.

As significant as the quantitative assessment of the Mennonite schools is the general impression. When the presidents of the Mennonite schools were asked to reflect on the challenges ahead, a

---

[17]For some of the smaller Canadian schools direct church subsidy represents a major portion of the budget. For example, both Aylmer Bible Institute and Institute Biblique Laval received half of their budget from the church. On the other side, US liberal arts colleges tend to receive 1% or less of their budgets directly from the church.

[18]If Bluffton and Fresno Pacific, the two schools with the most number of non-Mennonites on faculty, are excluded this increases to 83%.

[19]Cuninggim considers this mark "serious, onerous and mischievous," 43.

[20]The student bodies at Bluffton and Fresno Pacific are around 10% Mennonite. Conrad Grebel and Menno Simons are located on the campuses of public universities and so the dynamics are quite different.

[21]See the study of enrolment at Mennonite colleges by Leo Driedger, "Monastery or Marketplace?: Changing Mennonite College/Seminary Enrollments," *Journal of Mennonite Studies,* 15 (1997): 56-79.

significant number remarked on the need to strengthen the partnership with the supporting church body, or the need to find faculty who were integrally bound to the Anabaptist tradition. Personal conversations with the leaders of the schools only enforced this impression. The Mennonite identity of a college is not something which can ever be taken care of once and for all. But at the present time our Mennonite schools are very Mennonite. This conclusion is suggested by an appraisal of the schools with the use of formal criteria, and it is strongly supported by the comments and aspirations of those at the schools.

Mennonite school distinctives. I have suggested that our Mennonite post-secondary schools are very Mennonite. But what is the impact of this on the ethos and emphases of the college or seminary? Rod Sawatsky has suggested six contributions the Mennonite tradition can make to the world of Christian higher education.[22] The following is a brief summary of these, together with some specific examples of these from our schools.

1) Anabaptist-Mennonite incarnational ecclesiology. Mennonite colleges attempt to be incarnational, even as the church is incarnational. They advocate and model this by emphasizing that, the Word became flesh within the world, and through serving the world in the name of Christ. Mennonite colleges are called to nurture citizens of God's kingdom rather than of the nation. This ecclesiology implies some degree of church-world dualism. It thus has tended to shape ethnic or sectarian communties. The strong connections with and commitment to the church of virtually all Mennonite schools is just one example of this.

2) The ethic of Jesus. Ethics, or Christian discipleship, gives body to the Word at Mennonite colleges. Service and peacemaking are two key elements of this ethic. The emphasis on ethics in our Mennonite schools is reflected in the number of courses offered in ethics, and in the attention given to ethics in the various professional programs. The two specifics mentioned, service and peacemaking, are very prominent at Mennonite schools. Menno Simons, the institution least connected on a formal level to the Mennonite church, consists exclusively of two programs, one in conflict resolution and one in international

---

[22]Rod Sawatsky, "What Can the Mennonite Tradition Contribute to Christian Higher Education?" in *Models for Christian Higher Education: Strategies for Success in the Twenty-first Century*, Richard T. Hughes and William B. Adrain, eds. (Grand Rapids, MI: Eerdmans Publishing Company, 1997), 187-199.

development. In addition, at least Eastern Mennonite, Conrad Grebel and Fresno Pacific also have distinct programs in conflict resolution. CMBC has a program in service education. At Bluffton, an emphasis on peace and service have become major carriers of the Mennonite identity. No doubt many other examples could be given. The ethic of Jesus, especially as represented in an emphasis on peace and service, are signs of the Mennonite identity of our schools.

3) Internationalism. The church, as the incarnate body of Christ living according to Jesus' ethic, is a global community. Again, this tradition is alive and well at the Mennonite colleges. Perhaps the most obvious example is Goshen's ground breaking Study-Service Term (SST) program. Through this program more than five and a half thousand Goshen students have been introduced to the larger world in 15 different countries. Many other colleges have developed their own programs with a similar goal.

4) Biblical authority. Because the Bible is the authoritative text for Mennonites, it is the primary source of theological reflection in Mennonite colleges. One public manifestation of this is the names Mennonites have given some of their schools. Two of the seminaries include the word "biblical" in them, and seven of the schools in Canada continue to use the word "Bible" in their name.[23] More significantly, however, this emphasis is also reflected in the courses required and offered by most of the schools, including the liberal arts colleges.

5) Music. Music has always had a prominent place in Mennonite worship and celebration. Mennonite colleges thus have developed a strong musical tradition, especially in choral music. In the liberal arts colleges the music programs have been strong. Perhaps more strikingly,

---

[23] This observation, however, raises a troubling question as well. Swift Current Bible Institute is not included on this list because it closed its doors in the summer of 1996. Winkler Bible Institute is included, but it also closed its doors in the summer of 1997, just as this consultation was taking place. Aylmer Bible Institute is struggling, with the very real possibility that it will also not be able to continue. Concord College was Mennonite Brethren Bible College until recently when it changed its name. It should be added that a number of the schools with "Bible" in their name continue with strong enrolments (note especially Columbia Bible College). Nevertheless it does raise the question whether the traditional Mennonite conviction that the study of the Bible is foundational for the Christian life is flagging. A significant question for all Mennonite institutions in the future will need to be how the theological commitment Mennonites have to the authority of scripture is expressed in the structures, curricula and programs of its schools.

even the Bible colleges which have given limited attention to the arts in general, tend to have significant music programs.[24]

6) Communitarianism. Anabaptism may be considered a "lay monastic" movement, a movement of the common people. A consequence is the belief that all need to be educated to use their gifts fully in the service of God and community. Compared to other colleges at least, Mennonite colleges thus have tended not to emphasize individual achievement, but rather to speak of responsibility and service. Mennonite colleges attempt to build a communitarian spirit. They seek to model the notion of community.

Upward and onward, or rising to meet the challenge. Mennonites may have been slow to become involved in the academic game. Our traditional suspicion of higher education held us back. But once we became involved, we have pursued it with tremendous drive and passion. We have become competitive, aggressive, and ambitious, and at some points, even quite flexible. Here are some ways in which we have been changing, especially in the past decade or two. It may be debated whether these moves represent our adapting in order to survive within a rapidly changing marketplace, or whether the shifts are motivated more by vision or ambition.

1) Adaptation of programming. Mennonites have been creative and aggressive in adapting programs in response to pressures and opportunities. Graduate programs are added, and under-graduate programs evolve, in most cases becoming more professional in orientation. Fresno Pacific may serve as the clearest example of both of these. It began in 1944 as a fairly traditional Bible school. When enrolment pressures came it developed into a junior college. By 1965 it had become a fully accredited 4-year liberal arts college. In 1975 it initiated the first Mennonite college graduate programs. By now it has masters programs in education (with 15 areas of specialization), TESOL, administrative leadership and conflict management and peacemaking. Approximately 50% of its students are in these graduate programs, representing nearly one-third of its full-time equivalent enrolment. In a relatively short period of time it has evolved from a Bible institute to liberal arts college to a university with graduate

---

[24]Concord and CMBC, for example, have historically given primary place to biblical/theological studies. Nevertheless it has simply been assumed that these would be supplemented by a strong program in church music.

programs specializing in professional training.[25]

No other Mennonite school has such a dramatic history in this respect, but the approach of Fresno Pacific is not unique, even if it may have been pursued more aggressively in that context. A number of Mennonite institutions have added graduate programs, or participate in them. Eastern Mennonite has developed masters programs in education, counselling, and conflict transformation. Bluffton has also developed a masters program in education. Conrad Grebel has added the Master of Theological Studies degree. CMBC and Concord participate in a seminary consortium in Winnipeg. AMBS is considering adding a Doctor of Ministry program. The only Mennonite institution actively involved in doctoral level programming, Toronto Mennonite Theological Centre, also happens to be the youngest of all Mennonite post-secondary schools.

The change in undergraduate programs is equally striking. Some years ago Hesston was on the forefront of junior colleges emphasizing 2-year professional programs. The introduction of degree completion programs (with Bluffton a good example) represents an effort to be more flexible and reach a new market. Increased emphasis on professional programs is a response to a student market which tends to de-emphasize general education over against job preparation. At Bluffton the major with highest enrolment is organizational management; at Bethel and Hesston it is nursing. Traditional liberal arts majors (e.g., english, history, sociology) are far down the list. Even the recent popularity of programs in conflict resolution may be understood in the context of a movement away from general liberal arts education to programs perceived as having a more practical application.[26]

---

[25]See the fascinating story of this development in John Howard Yoder, "From Monastery to Marketplace: Idea and Mission in Graduate and Professional Programs at Fresno Pacific College," in *Mennonite Idealism and Higher Education: The Story of the Fresno Pacific College Idea*, ed. Paul Toews (Fresno, CA: Center for Mennonite Brethren Studies, 1995),133-151.

[26]The dynamics at Hesston and Fresno Pacific are interesting in this light. Although Fresno Pacific has developed the largest professional graduate programs of any Mennonite institution, its undergraduate program may very well have been less affected by the drive toward professional majors. A perusal of its recent graduates indicates that most majored in traditional liberal arts disciplines. Hesston, after developing a reputation as the Mennonite school with the 2-year professional programs, has returned more to a "junior college" approach in which the majority of its 2-year graduates continue their studies

2) Name Changes.
   Eastern Mennonite College – Eastern Mennonite Univeristy
   Pacific Bible Institute – Fresno Pacific College – Fresno Pacific
      University
   Steinbach Bible Institute – Steinbach Bible College
   Columbia Bible Institute – Columbia Bible College
   Mennonite Brethren Bible College – Concord College

3) The Accreditation of Bible Institutes. Recognition, or accreditation, have been significant factors for Mennonite schools for most of their history. Mennonite US liberal arts colleges and seminaries are all accredited by their regional accrediting associations, as well as by national professional bodies. When CMBC was founded in 1947 part of the vision was that it would relate to a public university. This aspect of the vision became reality in 1964 when it was designated An Approved Teaching Centre of the University of Manitoba. Mennonite Brethren Bible College (the forerunner of Concord) established a comparable relationship with the University of Winnipeg.

A similar dynamic appears to be at work among the Bible schools/institutes/colleges. Columbia and Steinbach have recently received their full accreditation by the Accrediting Association of Bible Colleges. Bethany and Rosedale are in the process of applying for this accreditation. The Institut Biblique Laval has developed a relationship with the University of Montreal. Formal recognition as schools and academic recognition for courses appear to be major concerns throughout.

In his article on Fresno Pacific, John Yoder[27] speaks of the movement from monastery to marketplace. Perhaps a critical question is how the Mennonite distinctives outlined above stand up as we adapt to the marketplace.

4) Time of Transition. A number of indicators suggest Mennonite schools are in a critical time of transition. Anecdotal evidence suggests that this is true of faculty at the schools. Two CMBC faculty retirements perhaps represent this change. Esther Wiebe and Waldemar Janzen began teaching at CMBC in 1954 and 1956 respectively. They were key figures in the school during the late 1950s and early 1960s when an identity and vision of the college was developed which has remained central to this time. Now they are retiring after a combined 83 years of service. New faculty will be hired, and new perspectives will

---

at 4-year colleges and universities.
[27]"From Monastery to Marketplace."

be contributed. A "changing of the guard" is taking place. This is one example from CMBC, but my impression from conversations with deans and presidents of other Mennonite colleges is that this is not unique but typical.

Nowhere is this transition as obvious as in the leadership positions of our Mennonite institutions. On July 1, 1997 the average tenure of the president at the following schools is approximately one year: AMBS, Bethany, Bethel, Bluffton, CMBC, Concord, Conrad Grebel, Fresno Pacific, Goshen, and Tabor.[28] Loren Schwartzentruber at Hesston, with four years of experience, is one of the senior presidents. Walter Unger at Columbia (1978) and Joe Lapp at Eastern Mennonite (1983) both have more seniority than the presidents of eleven of the schools combined.

But compared to the academic deans the presidents are still fairly experienced. This summer alone (1997) at least eight Mennonite colleges and seminaries will initiate new academic deans: Bethel, Bluffton, CMBC, Columbia, Concord, Goshen, Hesston, and Steinbach. In addition AMBS, Bethany, Fresno Pacific, MBBS, and Tabor have made changes recently;[29] that is, 13 changes since 1995. Given that some of the smaller schools may not have deans (and given that I do not have complete information on all Mennonite schools) it appears a nearly total change is taking place in the academic leadership of Mennonite schools. The church owners, and their boards may represent stability, but transition is the prevailing reality at least in the internal leadership of the Mennonite schools, and possibly within the faculties as well.

Canadian Schools Compared With US Schools The

---

[28]The following is a list of recent changes in the presidential office: Bethel –Douglas Penner (1995); Bethany–Doug Berg (1995); Tabor–David Brandt (1995); Conrad Grebel–John E. Toews (1996); Bluffton–Lee Snyder (1996); Goshen–Shirley Showalter (1996); AMBS–Nelson Kraybill (1997); CMBC –Gerald Gerbrandt (1997); Concord–Harry Olfert (1997); Fresno Pacific– Allen Carden (1997).

[29]The following is a list of recent changes in the dean's office: AMBS– Willard Swartley (1996); Fresno Pacific–Howard Loewen (1996); MBBS– Pierre Gilbert (1996); Columbia–Ron Penner (1997); Steinbach–Don Thiessen (1997); CMBC–John J. Friesen (1997); Concord–Dave Dyck (1997); Goshen–Paul Keim (1997); Hesston–Bonnie Sowers (1997); Bethel –John Sheriff (1997); Bluffton–John Kampen (1997).

recently published *Models for Christian Higher Education*[30] is a fine example of a study of Christian higher education. It is, however, exclusively devoted to schools located in the US. Having studied and worked on both sides of the border has emphasized for me how different the two worlds are. Given that nearly half of Mennonite post-secondary schools in North America are located in Canada, it becomes important for any understanding of Mennonite higher education to be aware of the differences in these two worlds. It might also be suggested that such an introduction to these differences is especially important for those of us working in US Mennonite schools. For the reality is that most Canadian Mennonites involved in higher education have had experience in US schools, and so they are well aware of the difference, whereas relatively few US Mennonites involved in higher education have had the opportunity of either studying or working in Canadian schools.

It is impossible within the parameters of this presentation to do a careful study of the differences between the two countries, either within the larger educational context or within our Mennonite post-secondary schools. The following is a list of suggested differences, some based on hard data, while others arise out of personal experience and impression. I expect a more systematic study would confirm most observations although possibly raise questions about some. Nevertheless I trust they will be helpful.

Differences in the national educational context. An American examining Mennonite higher education in Canada will quickly notice that Canadian Mennonite schools have been significantly affected or influenced by higher education trends in Canada. Undoubtedly the same is true of Mennonite schools in the US. It thus becomes necessary to make some observations on the differences.

1) The near absence of liberal arts colleges in Canada. The Canadian higher education scene is dominated by two types of institutions: large, public universities, and community colleges with professional or vocational programs.[31] In some provinces the sharp line between these

---

[30]Richard T. Hughes and William B. Adrian, eds. (Grand Rapids, MI: Eerdmans Publishing Company, 1997).

[31]Manitoba, for example, has three public universities (University of Manitoba, University of Winnipeg, and Brandon University), and a few smaller, regional community colleges. University of Winnipeg and Brandon University began as church-related colleges, but became public universities many years ago. Saskatchewan has two public universities (University of

two has become quite fuzzy, and in all provinces there is more cross-over between the two. Earlier in this century there were also a number of church colleges, but these either became public universities, or were absorbed into them. The exceptions to this are the many small Bible "schools," found especially in western Canada but not entirely absent in the east.[32]

The liberal arts college, so prevalent throughout the US, both church-run as well as semi-public, was a rare breed in Canada. The last few years have seen a few develop, but even now there are only seven or so which would truly compare with the US liberal arts college.[33]

2) Greater compartmentalization of education. The absence of the liberal arts college has resulted in a greater compartamentalization of education. At the risk of over-simplifying it might be suggested that higher education in Canada has consisted of four types: a) arts and sciences faculties within the university—there may be some similarity between these and the liberal arts colleges, but seldom do these faculties have the vision for the education of the whole person so significant in the liberal arts college; b) professional faculties within the university—nursing, social work, management, law, engineering, etc. are all separate faculties within the university, frequently with very limited contact general arts and sciences; c) vocationally oriented community colleges; d) biblical/theological studies in the church Bible institutions. It should be added that although this has been the case, there is significant change taking place as the new liberal arts colleges develop, and the church Bible institutions add programs more like those of a liberal arts college.

3) Lower level of participation in post-secondary education. Although since the Second World War there has also been significant

---

Saskatchewan and Regina University) and a number of regional community colleges.

[32]Manitoba, a few years ago, had at least the following: CMBC, Mennonite Brethren Bible College, Canadian Nazarene College, Catharine Booth Bible College, Winnipeg Bible College, Steinbach Bible Institute, Elim Bible Institute, and Winkler Bible Institute. In addition there were probably a few more which never became part of the higher education dialogue in Manitoba. Saskatchewan and Alberta each have many more.

[33]British Columbia: Trinity Western (Free Church); Alberta: The King's University College (Christian Reformed), Augustana College (Lutheran), Concordia College (Lutheran), Canadian Union College (Seventh Day Adventist); Ontario: Redeemer College (Christian Reformed); New Brunswick: Atlantic Baptist College Canada (Baptist).

growth in the higher education scene in Canada nevertheless, a much lower portion of Canadian young people attend university.

4) Financial reality is very different. The financial realities of Canadian higher education is very different from the US. At least three differences can be noted: a) Philanthropy of higher education is much less common in Canada. There is no University of Chicago, or Duke, both schools founded largely through the gifts of some individual. In Canada higher education has been funded primarily by governments. b) The much greater wealth of the US is very evident when the campuses of US schools are compared with those of Canadian. c) Tuition at Canadian schools is much lower than in the US.

5) Lesser emphasis on athletics. This difference may not be as significant as the others, but it is more visible, and in some ways represents the very different style of Canadian higher education. For example, the football program at the University of Manitoba (the largest university in Manitoba with some 25,000 students) probably receives considerably less emphasis than that of Bluffton or Bethel. Attendance at games will be much less than at Bluffton or Bethel; there are no athletic scholarships; the coaching staff is small, etc.

Differences between the Mennonite schools. Here I cite the following differences.

1) Prevalence of Bible schools and colleges. This may be the most visible of the differences. Eight of the eleven schools listed in Canada began as Bible schools or Bible colleges. It is recognized that such schools are not unique to Canada, but they have remained much more significant. H. S. Bender names 40 Bible schools started by Mennonites between 1886 and 1950 of which 15 were in the US.[34] Walter Unger names 40 started in western Canada alone between 1900 and 1940.[35] The Bible school movement has had a much more significant impact in Canada in general, and among Canadian Mennonites in particular.

2) More direct ownership by the church body. Most Canadian Mennonite post-secondary schools were founded by the church, and most schools continue to be wholly owned and operated by a Mennonite conference. The board of directors is elected by the church body, and the church body participates in key program decisions. The schools are part of budget of the conference.

3) More positive attitude toward the government and the public education system. Canadian Mennonite post-secondary schools have

---

[34]H. S. Bender, "Bible School," *Mennonite Encyclopedia.*

[35]Walter Unger, "Bible Colleges and Institutes," *Mennonite Encyclopedia.*

not been established over against, or as an alternative to the public school system, but as supplementary to them. The early Bible schools had a very distinct purpose: biblical education and the preparation of church workers. Later schools were started with the assumption that they would have a relationship to the university. Even before CMBC had offered its first classes in the fall of 1947 the vision was to relate to the university. In 1964 it became An Approved Teaching Centre of the University of Manitoba. Mennonite Brethren Bible College (and the Canadian Nazarene College) were not far behind. A number of other Bible schools and Bible colleges have worked on similar relationships in the past decade or so.

More recently, Mennonites in Canada have established two institutions right on the university campus. In 1964 Conrad Grebel became one of a number of church colleges on the University of Waterloo campus. It emphasizes a residential community, and offers a broad range of courses in number of programs for Waterloo students. Some 25 years later Menno Simons College became the second Mennonite institution on a public university campus. Both schools have appreciated the university setting, and have made a valuable contribution to those universities.

This different approach to the public sphere has also contributed to making Canadian schools much more open to working with the government and to receiving government support. Conrad Grebel, as part of the University of Waterloo, is an integral part of the Ontario university system. In this manner it has received over $800,000 annually from the government, an amount representing approximately 30% of its operating budget. CMBC, Concord, Menno Simons and Steinbach all receive government subsidy as well, although at present at a much lower level.[36] Many other examples could be given exemplifying the different relationship between church school and government or public education in Canada.

4) Tremendous ferment. Canadian Mennonite schools are in a time of tremendous ferment. Winkler and Swift Current have closed because of insufficient enrolment. Aylmer is considering such a possibility. Columbia and Steinbach have become Bible colleges. Mennonite Brethren Bible College has become Concord College. CMBC, Concord and Menno Simons are negotiating a possible federation which would produce an institution much more like an American liberal arts college than any other present Mennonite institution in Canada.

---

[36]See *supra*, n.11.

Conclusion It is easy to highlight differences between various Mennonite schools. Small Bible schools like Winkler, Aylmer, and the Institut Biblique Laval may at first glance have little in common with the large Mennonite universities in Harrisonburg or Fresno. And yet the commonalties are great. I expect that the Anabaptist distinctives suggested by Rod Sawatsky[37] will be present in each of the schools, even if in somewhat different styles. My conversations with the school leaders, and my reading in the various types of literature produced by the schools, suggest that our Mennonite post-secondary institutions are very Mennonite, struggling with how to bring together the following four convictions or realities:

Our commitment to Anabaptism. The commitment to Anabaptism is visibly evident in what the schools say about themselves, and how they look towards the future. Theological and philosophical debates about what it means to be a Mennonite school are common. The following questions are regularly asked in a number of the schools: Do the board members all need to be Mennonite? Do the faculty all need to be Mennonite? Is there a certain percentage of the student body which needs to be Mennonite to quality as a Mennonite college? What are the key aspects of Anabaptism which need to be emphasized in a Mennonite college? The vitality of the debate on these issues is but one sign of the commitment to remaining Anabaptist. I was struck by the number of presidents who responded that their greatest challenge in the years ahead was to strengthen their tie to the Mennonite community. We may not have the same sense for what it means to be a Mennonite institution, but there is a common commitment that that is what we want to be.

The need to remain viable. Schools without sufficient student numbers or financial support die—that is the reality of educational institutions. It has been suggested that all colleges and seminaries are only three or four years away from extinction. Maintaining viable student numbers and strong financial support is an increasing challenge in a time of tremendous competition for students, tight economics, and decreasing loyalty to church denominations. Each school thus is forced to ask what kind of adaptations are required in order to remain viable.

The mandate to nurture the church's youth and develop leadership for the church. All of the church's colleges include in their mandate the task of nurturing the youth of the church, as well as of participating in the task of preparing leaders for the church. For the seminaries this

---

[37]See *supra*, n.21.

latter task becomes the primary one. In each of these contexts, however, the challenge of how to do this most effectively is present. What is the right balance between affirming the faith and raising critical questions? What kind of curriculum serves this goal best? How does the institution structure non-curricular learning? Again, the method chosen or deemed best in the various settings may differ, but the overall commitment to this task is there.

The biblical invitation to serve others. The motto of Goshen is "Culture for Service." In this word "service" we have an Anabaptist distinctive, and the sense that no school should serve only itself, its students, or even its supporting church body. Do the schools do this only by preparing students to serve beyond the Mennonite communities? Or do the schools themselves participate in this mission? It is interesting to observe how the way different institutions respond to this task is influenced by factors such as geographical location,[38] church tradition,[39] viability, and history of the school.

----

[38]Perhaps not surprisingly, the more urban the context in which the school is located, the more likely it is to stress its mission beyond the Mennonite community. The one exception to this is Bluffton College, a school located in a small town in rural Ohio, but also a school with a relatively small Mennonite supporting body. Viability thus forces a school like Bluffton to reach out. "Necessity becomes the mother of invention."

[39]I have the impression that the Mennonite Brethren emphasis on evangelism has influenced the Mennonite Brethren schools to place greater weight on reaching out to non-Mennonite students.

3 Mennonite Youth (Part I)

Abe Bergen[1]

Introduction I recently found the following description of "our generation" on the Internet[2]

We are the children of the eighties. We are not the first "lost generation" nor today's lost generation. In fact, we think we know just where we stand—or are discovering it as we speak. We are the ones who played with Lego Building Blocks when they were just building blocks and gave Malibu Barbie crewcuts with safety scissors that never really cut. We collected Garbage Pail Kids and Cabbage Patch Kids and My Little Ponies and Hot Wheels and He-Man action figures and She-Ra looked just a little bit like a woman. Big wheels and bicycles with streamers were the way to go, and sidewalk chalk was all you needed to build a city. Imagination was the key. It made the Ewok Tree house big enough for you to be Luke and the kitchen table and an old sheet dark enough to be a tent in the forest. Your world was the backyard and it was all you needed. With your pink portable tape player, Debbie Gibson sang back up to you and everyone wanted a skirt like the Material Girl and a glove like Michael Jackson's. Today we are the ones who sing along with Bruce Springsteen and the Bangles perfectly and have no idea why. We recite lines with the Ghostbusters and still look to The Goonies for a great adventure. We flip through TV stations and stop at The A-Team and Knight Rider and Fame and laugh with The Cosby Show and Family Ties and Punky Brewster and what you talking about Willis? We hold strong affections for The Muppets and The Gummy Bears and why did they take The Smurfs off the air? After school specials were only about cigarettes and step-families, the Pokka Dot Door and nothing like Barney, and aren't the Power Rangers just Voltron reincarnated? We are the ones

---

[1]Director of Youth Ministry, the General Conference Mennonite Church and part-time teacher in Practical Theology, Canadian Mennonite Bible College.

[2]From the Internet (1/16/97)

who read Nancy Drew and the Hardy Boys, the Bobbsey Twins, Beverly Cleary and Judy Blume, Richard Scary and the Electric Company. Friendship bracelets were ties you couldn't break and friendship pins went on shoes—preferably high top Velcro Reebok—and pegged jeans were in, as were Units belts and layered socks and jean jackets and jams and charm necklaces and side pony tails and just tails. Rave was a girl's best friend; braces with colored rubber bands made you cool. The backdoor was always open and Mom served only red Kool-Aid to the neighborhood kids—never drank New Coke. Entertainment was cheap and lasted for hours. All you need to be a princess was high heels and an apron; the Sit'n'Spin always made you dizzy but never made you stop; Pogo balls were dangerous weapons and Chinese Jump Ropes never failed to trip someone. In your Underoos you were Wonder Woman or Spider Man or R2D2 and in your tree house you were king. In the Eighties, nothing was wrong. Did you know the president was shot? Star Wars was not only a movie. Did you ever play in a bomb shelter? Did you see the Challenger explode or feed the homeless man? We forgot Vietnam and watched Tiananmen's Square on CNN and bought pieces of the Berlin Wall at the store. Aids was not the number one killer in the United States. We didn't start the fire, Billy Joel. In the Eighties, we redefined the American Dream, and those years defined us. We are the generation in between the strife and not turning our backs. The Eighties may have made us idealistic, but it's that idealism that will push us and be passed on to our children—the first children of the twenty-first century. Never forget: We are the children of the Eighties. If this is familiar, you are one of us . . . pass it on to all the others . . .

Dave

General Cultural Shifts and Trends It is impossible to adequately describe the generation that is now in high school and moving into college. In the above written description, Dave attempts to describe his generation, naming many common growing-up experiences and life-shaping influences. As some events such as the assassination of John F. Kennedy and Neil Armstrong's walk on the moon became defining moments for the baby boomers, so the coming down of the Berlin wall and the explosion of the Challenger, among others, have become defining moments for the children of the boomers, the baby busters.

Another way to describe this generation is to examine some of the cultural shifts and trends that have taken place during the past decade. Generalizations made about the baby busters or the baby echo generation (usually referred to as the Millennial kids in the US) will simply identify larger societal trends as observed by sociologists and trend watchers. These descriptions will be unfair for some and barely adequate for most.

Young people do not evolve in a social vacuum. They are shaped by complex and multifaceted forces beyond their control. These include parents, peers, the media as well as other more general societal forces. The following cultural shifts are impacting the lives of youth in significant ways.

Youth Culture has shifted from a monolithic culture to sub-populations. One of the reasons it is difficult to describe youth today is because youth culture has become complex. According to Mark Senter,[3] when baby boomers were growing up, youth were part of a fairly simple social system. On the top of the heap were the "jocks" and the "rah-rahs" (cheerleaders). These were the popular kids that everyone looked up to and aspired to be like. They were the somebodies. Most of the rest were "wannabees." They wanted to be noticed and known, and tried to be popular by doing well academically, becoming involved in the yearbook committee, or the drama club, or the school band, only to discover that none of these involvements paved the way to popularity.

At the bottom rung were the drop-outs or the "greasers." They did not care about being popular and received their attention through negative social behaviours. Many were in trouble with the law, consumed alcohol and some used drugs. This three-tiered structure reflected a fairly simple social system.

Today the structure is more complex. In school, for example, we now have many small groupings having little to do with each other. These sub-populations were formed as a result of shared interests of the youth. There are still jocks around, only now they are not on the top rung of the social latter, nor is everyone aspiring to become one. Instead, an important aspect for youth is simply being able to belong to a friendship group that accepts them. Some of these sub-populations include groups such as preppies, hackers, skaters, geeks, druggies, nerds . . . and the list goes on. These sub-populations co-exist and to a great extent allow each other "to be" without too much hassle or harassment. These groups who live in different worlds are difficult to bring together for a common purpose. Most would rather simply "hang out" with their chosen friendship clusters and not bother with other groups.

Young people have never been more informed. It is popular for teachers and professors to complain that young people are not as

---

[3]Mark H. Senter III, "Trickle-Down Strategies Come to an End," *Youthworker* (Summer 1994): 38-44.

knowledgeable as their parents or grandparents were when they were teenagers. Such an observation is usually made by an instructor who has just graded a paper that has exhibited poor writing skills. It may be that readin', writin', and 'rithmatic skills are not as highly developed in today's teens as a generation or two ago. However, according to Bibby and Posterski, "today's young people are the best informed teenagers in Canadian history,"[4] especially when it comes to basic awareness of what's happening in the world.

Their awareness in not the result of book learning, "but because of today's three Ts—television, technology and travel."[5] Television has changed the way life is seen and interpreted. An unlimited number of channels available to teens allows them to experience world events as they are happening. They watched a real war (Gulf War) on CNN and were brought "face to face" with the starving people of Ethiopia.

Since more hours are spent watching TV than anything else, they are impacted in other ways as well. MTV claims they "own" young people, alleging they influence their attitudes, what they buy, the kind of music they listen to and much more. Other television shows have power to influence values and behaviour. Situation comedies often portray lifestyles that are in contradiction with Christian values. By watching many hours of such shows, Christian values are constantly challenged and undermined. By the time they are eighteen, some have seen more sexual fantasies enacted on the screen than their grandparents ever thought about or experienced in a lifetime.

Besides being able to surf 20 to 50 channels most times of the day or night, it is not unusual for them to watch two or three movies on a weekend evening. They experience much of life through the tube. Many teens know more about the personal lives of their Hollywood heroes than they do about extended family members.

Technology has contributed to the information explosion—VCRs, CDs, and computers which give access to the Internet make it possible to access more information than ever thought possible. An entire encyclopedia can be stored on a single CD-Rom. By searching the Internet, it is possible to find hundreds of articles on any conceivable topic imaginable.

Our society moved from the industrial age to the quantum age where information doubles every four years. In the quantum age, there is not

---

[4]Reginald W. Bibby and Donald C. Posterski, *Teen Trends* (Toronto: Stoddart Publishing, 1992), 60.

[5]Ibid., 61.

only more information, it is also necessary to learn different ways of thinking. Linear thinking is replaced with interactive thought. This means there is no longer simply cause and effect, but rather "potentials" depending on how someone or something comes into relationship with the event. Every situation has many potential results. In the industrial age chaos was to be avoided, but in the quantum age chaos leads to a new order. Networks become more important than hierarchy.

The quantum age requires a new way of thinking and new skills for dealing with the information. These are the skills teens need to learn in order to deal with technology they use everyday. They are learning these skills without resistance, much more rapidly than older generations are able to.

Young people are also learning a lot through travel. They are not only travelling outside of their provinces/states, but outside of their countries. It is common for high school students from Canada or the United States to spend a week or two in Europe or even to live in another country as an exchange student for three to nine months. Living in another cultural context affords many opportunities for broadening perspectives and understanding.

Affluence, which permits this kind of travel, television and technology, has put young people in direct contact with other parts of the world, have expanded their world views and has given young people a greater knowledge and awareness of the world they live in than previous generations.

Math and literacy skills may not be as highly developed in teens today as they were thirty years ago. However, society does not depend on written work and math skills in the way it used to. There are different ways of obtaining and storing information than in the past. Calculators and computers allow us to depend less on what we can store in our heads or are able to compute mentally. Those who are concerned with young people's declining abilities in the traditional 3 Rs need to temper that with a recognition that currently young people are learning many new skills which equip them to survive in today's world. They need to know where to get information and how to deal with it, rather than memorize it. The skills of interpretation and discernment are ones that educational institutions need to enhance so that teens will have the ability to know what to do with the information they access.

Young people live with many stresses and pressures but remain optimistic. The global village in which young people grow up has made youth aware of the many crises and problems that exist. Everyone is trying to convince youth of the urgency of their causes and hence teenagers are likely to see serious problems everywhere. AIDS is seen by many as a threat and other social concerns are seen as being more serious than they were eight years earlier.

THE MAJOR SOCIAL CONCERNS[6]
% indicating very serious

	1984	1992
AIDS	--	77
Environment	37	69
Child Abuse	50	64
Drugs	46	64
Teenage Suicide	41	59

Not only are teens keenly aware of the problems around them, they are personally affected by them. Many know other teens personally who have been abused (40%), someone who has a serious drug or alcohol problem (62%), someone who has attempted suicide (60%). Females are more likely than males to have this personal knowledge.[7] Other issues of serious concern are racial discrimination, violence against women, and the economy. More recently, youth gangs and school violence have reached a serious stage.

With regard to personal concerns, the pressure to do well at school, the feeling of never having enough time, lack of money and wondering what they will do when they graduate are dominant. They worry about losing friends (including romantic partners) and not being understood by parents.[8]

Teens also feel pressure to have a perfect body. Through the media, magazines, television and advertising, they are constantly bombarded with images of gorgeous models. The pictures in magazines who show women who are slim with beautiful figures and flawless complexions. The men they see in ads are athletic with muscular biceps and great skin tone. The subtle message that is constantly sent to every teen is: "You

---

[6]Ibid., 76.

[7]Ibid., 78.

[8]Ibid., 88.

don't measure up, you're flawed." In pursuit of the perfect body, many girls get caught up in eating disorders or suffer low self esteem and depression when they realize they are not able to measure up to this perfect image. Boys may be tempted to try steroids in order to build up their bodies more quickly.

The temptation to base one's personal worth on outward appearance is perpetuated further by the clothing industry. A majority of teens feel pressure to buy expensive designer clothing in order to be popular or feel accepted by their peers. This results in paying two or three times the amount for similar quality clothing items which may not have the right label sewn into them. The pressure to spend a lot of money on clothing can create tensions in the home when family budgets cannot meet the demands, or it may result in teens taking on part-time jobs while trying to keep up with a full load of courses at school.

While crises surround them and problems loom large, young people continue to expect good fortunes and anticipate a better lifestyle than their parents. They dream big:

> 60 % expect to graduate from university.
> 75% expect to be better off than their parents.
> 95 % expect to own their own homes.
> 85% expect to stay married to the same person for life.[9]

Driedger and Bergen found this optimism in a recent church-wide study.[10]

---

[9]Ibid., 109.

[10]Leo Driedger and Abe Bergen, "Growing Roots and Wings: The Emergence of Mennonite Teens," *Journal of Mennonite Studies* 13 (1995): 153.

Assessment of Individual Strengths and Weaknesses, by Teens	Total Sample N==3795	GC N=307	MC N-326
Which Phrases Accurately Describe You?	Percentages		
Positive			
Have high hopes	87	85	89
Reliable	86	89	90
Respected by others	86	90	91
An achiever	80	81	79
Religious	78	79	75
Seeking answers	74	80	77
Encouraged	74	69	80
Upbeat	63	61	66
Physically attractive	61	58	68
High integrity	60	66	67
Content	59	65	69
Negative			
Confused	55	58	51
Too busy	54	55	51
Stressed out	50	51	45
Always tired	46	45	41
Lazy	41	38	39
Lonely	36	39	31
Disappointed	35	36	31
Skeptical	33	34	32
Mistrust people	32	30	29
Angry with life	26	23	20
Resentful	25	23	17
Unmotivated	20	18	22
Lacking purpose	20	22	20

Pressures and stresses are immense and keep mounting. Yet teens remain resilient as a group. Aware of world problems and crises, bombarded with pressures and stresses from many sources, they remain relatively hopeful about their future. Ideals remain high and dreams continue to motivate, stimulate and inspire. Will they be able to keep a balance between their realism and optimism? Will they have the supports and resources to continue when they encounter roadblocks and experience failures?

Mennonite Teens Mennonite teens are influenced by mainstream culture as much as their secular counterparts. However, they also enjoy supports, which counteract some of these pressures and result in more positive outcomes. The three assets that they benefit from are: a strong family system, positive life values and belief in God. These assets will be discussed further by examining the following three questions: Who are their families of origin? What do they value? How do they understand/experience God? Most of the data used comes from two sources: A study conducted by Barna Research Group that included both the General Conference and the Mennonite Church[11] and research done by Bibby and Posterski which was published in *Teen Trends*.

Who are their families of origin? In society we see many diverse forms of family—single parent households, blended or layered families, to mention a few. Mennonite families too have experienced divorce and remarriage, but the number of divorces remain relatively low when compared to general society. Mennonite youth are still more likely to live with their two biological parents (90% said they live with both biological parents). Mennonite teens may not have experienced the trauma of parents separating and divorcing, but they know about these experiences through their peers and through what they see in the media.

An alarming shift is found in the fact that youth spend little significant time with their parents. They are likely to spend at least two hours a day unsupervised by an adult. Two-career families have turned the energy of the home outward to places of work. Children often receive only left over time and energy. In a majority of families, including Mennonite families, children are likely to have less than an hour of meaningful conversation with parents per week. Young people report that they receive less enjoyment from family life than a decade

---

[11]The 1994 "Churched Youth Survey" was completed by the cooperation of the Josh McDowell Ministry, thirteen denominational leaders, and the Barna Research Group. The eight page survey questionnaire was pretested, and completed anonymously by 3,795 churched youth in late 1993 and early 1994. Each denomination was given the goal of surveying 500 youth from their total church list using a "multistage stratified random probability sample." Surveys were distributed and completed during a regular youth group meeting with no prior notice. Some of the research was published by Driedger and Bergen in "Growing Roots and Wings: Emergence of Mennonite Teens." A full copy of the survey results can be optained from the author.

ago. Consider the following chart:[12]

Teen-Parent Demonstrations of Love and Affection

	My Father			My Mother		
	Total	GC	MC	Total	GC	MC
Frequently	Percentages					
We are very/fairly close	74	79	79	88	86	91
Never wonder whether loves me	57	57	57	59	60	67
Spends 30 minutes plus with me						
Weekly on things that matter	34	36	37	53	62	51
Do something special together	19	13	16	30	22	17
Talk about personal concerns	12	10	9	39	31	33

Some things have not changed much during the past several decades.[13] Children, including youth, still spend much more time with mom than with dad. As a result they are more influenced by mom when making decisions, are likely to confide in mom about things that are important to them and will more likely go to mom when they have problems to discuss.

Greater mobility has isolated the nuclear family and left the role of parenting to one or two persons. As a result, many do not know members of their extended family and since they are not in geographical proximity, youth are not able to benefit from the support that the extended family has given in the past. Though extended family networks are still relatively strong within the Mennonite experience, similar isolation has occurred for many Mennonite families as well.

Despite the pressures and stresses that the families have experienced

---

[12]Ibid., 157.

[13]Similar results were found in a study conducted by Bernie Wiebe, *Self-Disclosure and Perceived Relationships of Mennonite Adolescents in Senior High School* (Ph.D. diss., University of North Dakota, 1974).

in the past decades, it remains a primary place where hearts and minds of children are shaped. Whatever size or grouping, the family continues to influence children more substantially than any other institution in society. While Mennonite families are also showing signs of stress, their resources still remain relatively strong. The support and guidance received by Mennonite youth from their parents remains a positive asset as they deal with daily pressures and decisions.

What do they value? Young people value friendships more than anything else, though there are noticeable shifts toward individualism. Bibby and Posterski found that, 84% viewed friendship as very important and in the Mennonite study, having close personal relationships was important to 89% of the youth. Despite the fact that friendship is highly valued and loyalty to friends must be maintained at all cost, there has been a drop in its importance during the past decade. Bibby and Posterski interpret this as a sign of accelerated individualism in Canadian society.[14]

Interpersonal values have also shifted toward individualism. They greatly value their freedom and independence and strive for personal goals of success and a comfortable life (70% of Mennonite youth said they wanted a comfortable lifestyle). Commitment to other interpersonal values such as honesty, forgiveness, and politeness has decreased. They are more concerned with looking after themselves at the expense of caring about others, or society in general. Consider the following chart:[15]

---

[14]Bibby and Posterski, 13.

[15]Driedger and Bergen, 151.

Values of North American Teens Aged 13-18			
How Desirable is (A lot)	Total	GC	MC
Primary Relationships	Percentages		
Having one marriage partner for life	85	86	89
Having close personal relationships	81	89	82
Having a close relationship with God	77	75	79
Having a spouse and children	73	73	70
High personal integrity	69	68	67
Having a fulfilled sex life within marriage	61	61	63
Living close to family	48	41	42
Secondary Relationships			
Influencing other people's lives	64	54	62
Being active in church	64	49	55
To make a difference in the world	62	55	53
Having a high-paying job	55	45	48

Values around parenthood show a similar trend. Ideals remain high when it comes to marriage—85% want to marry and expect to stay together (in both the Canadian and Mennonite surveys) but fewer want children than a decade ago (84%, down from 92%). This shift is not because women want careers, but because both men and women want more personal freedom (individualism). 95% of both males and females want to pursue a career when they have completed their education. There is more cohabitation, not as an alternative to marriage, but as something that precedes marriage, or takes place in between marriages.

Many are postponing marriage, but not sex. It is believed that 55% of teens in Canada (15-18 year olds) are sexually intimate.[16] Equally alarming is the fact that 87% said that "sex before marriage is alright when people love each other."[17] The sexual revolution has changed the way Canadians view sex outside of marriage. Here youth reflect their parents to a great extent.

Sexual intimacy for Mennonite youth is significantly less as the

---

[16]Bibby and Posterski, 39.

[17]Ibid., 42.

following table shows:[18]

Attitudes and Behavior of Teenagers with the Opposite Sex						
Which of the following are	Applicable if in Love			Have Done		
acceptable or have you done	Total	GC	MC	Total	GC	MC
with the opposite sex?						
	Percentages					
Held hands	85	90	88	89	82	89
Embrace and some kissing	68	73	69	73	64	67
Heavy "French" kissing	33	36	31	53	42	45
Fondling of breasts	10	10	9	34	34	31
Fondling of genitals	9	9	8	16	23	21
Sexual intercourse	7	6	5	16	8	8

While Mennonite teens do not measure up to their ideals in their sexual behaviour, the studies suggest they are significantly less sexually active than their secular counterparts. Their main criteria for having sex is based on whether they love each other, a personally subjective, individualistic value.

How do they understand/experience God? Bibby and Posterski found that youth believe in a personal God and view God as someone who understands "me" and is my "friend." In the *Churched Youth Study,* 75-80% said that having a close relationship with God was important to them. They feel closest to God in times of trouble: death of a friend, pet, family, or break-up with a boy/girlfriend. They also feel close to God when near nature and in special worship services. Their experience of God is primarily individualistic and subjective.

Individualism is evident in the fact that youth in society claim they get little enjoyment from attending church (only 30% in the Canadian study receive a great deal or quite a lot of enjoyment from attending church). Though 80% of Canadians still identify themselves with a major religious group while only 20% attend. In the Mennonite survey, 80% said they attended church, youth group or Sunday School once a week.

---

[18]Bergen and Driedger, 158.

Religious Beliefs and Activities of Teens			
Religious Beliefs and Behavior	Total	GC	MC
	Percentages		
Made a personal commitment to Jesus Christ still important	86	78	82
God is all-powerful, all-knowing creator who rules world today	85	84	85
Attend a church youth group weekly	84	83	82
Attend church services every week	82	78	86
Pray to God daily	65	67	67
Read the Bible every week or more	48	45	55

While the above study[19] did not take into account youth who had dropped out of church, it is clear that those who participate in the programs are committed to church involvement and fairly faithful in practicing spiritual disciplines.

Summary and Conclusion   Teenage life and spirituality is becoming more individualistic in an increasingly pluralistic society. For many, friendship circles are small and consist of homogenous sub-populations who do not necessarily want much to do with other groups that are different or do not share common interests. Teens are bombarded with information and opportunities, unprecedented in history, yet are not always certain how to deal with all the information they are given. As a generation they have inherited many major social problems which beg for solutions. These crises weigh heavily alongside the everyday pressures they face growing up as a teenager.

Daily they encounter different and competing philosophies and belief systems. Right and wrong for many have become a matter of opinion. When confronted by diverse philosophies or conflicting values systems, they are likely to pick and choose the things that are suitable to them or seem right to them, whether or not particular ideas fit into a coherent whole.

Teens have learned well from their parents and their culture—they

---

[19]Ibid., 159.

have bought into the individualism that is prevalent in society and are living their lives in greater isolation from their families and the institutions that have surrounded them in the past. They are more informed and educated, experience endless choices and options, but lack coherent value systems upon which to base their decisions. Increasingly they do not have the supports they need when experiencing a crisis or trying to deal with personal problems.

Mennonite teens have much in common with their secular counterparts. They will likely not differ much in the way they dress, the pressures they experience, the type of music they listen to, and the television shows they watch. For most, however, their family supports are more intact and extensive, and their behaviours are still more rooted in biblical values than their secular counterparts, particularly in the area of sexual attitudes and behaviours. Family and church continue to shape, influence and support them in their endeavours. However Mennonite families are also showing signs of stress as parents' lives get busier and only leftover time and energy remain for family life. They are spending little time together as families.

There is a further danger that church ties will also be weakening and that a greater percentage of Mennonite teens will become bored or disillusioned with the church unless programs of the church are kept vibrant and interesting. With strong family supports and solid connections to the church community, they can continue to be resilient in their response to the pressures and temptations of society and live counter-culturally in a way that is consistent with biblical teachings.

----

4 Mennonite Youth (Part II)

Ritch Hochstetler[1]

Introduction An apocryphal story of Jesus teaching his disciples the beatitudes goes like this:

> Then Jesus took his disciples up onto the mountain and gathering around him he taught them saying, "Blessed are the poor in Spirit, for theirs is the kingdom of heaven; Blessed are the meek; Blessed are they that mourn; Blessed are the merciful; Blessed are they that thirst for justice; Blessed are you when you are persecuted; Blessed are you when you suffer; Be glad and rejoice, for your reward is great in heaven." Then Simon Peter said, "Are we supposed to know this?" And Andrew said, "Do we have to write this down?" And James said, "Will we be tested on this?" And Bartholomew said, "Do we have to turn this in?" And John said, "The other disciples didn't have to learn this!" And Judas said, "What does this have to do with anything?" Then one of the Pharisees asked to see Jesus' lesson plan, and inquired of Jesus, "Where are your objectives in the cognitive domain?" And Jesus wept.

How often do we weep when working with adolescents who "just don't get it!" On the one hand, we believe that what we have to offer is essential to their own development and functioning in the world. On the other hand, it is a major task to find ways of getting their attention. My purpose in this paper is to ask, "Who are the Mennonite youth?" I will do this by looking at several of the complex and varied factors under the headings: cultural trends, what do kids value, and critical concerns. But first a warning: this journey is not for the faint of heart, for placing our youth under the microscope will require us to gaze deeply into the choices, successes, and failures of our own lives.

A starting point for "finding the pulse" of Mennonite youth is current social reality. I will describe the powerful cultural milieu kids are part

---

[1]Associate Pastor of Youth Ministry, Hesston Mennonite Church.

of today. I will also look ahead to what they may be facing in the not so distant future. It is important to note that there has been a significant shift in the composition of "youth culture" that was brought into existence with the creation of high schools, football games, dances, music, and assorted other cultural practices. The monolithic anti-establishment culture of the 1960s has given way to a dazzling array of multi-layered youth sub-cultures, each with its own rules, rites of passage, and defining characteristics. Nevertheless, even with this plethora of subcultures there are common threads that connect them together. Yet the best we can hope for is to try to get a sense of the underlying meanings of particular cultural distinctives and movements.

Cultural Trends There are three cultural trends that I want to identify. *First*, say hello to "The Fourth Turning: Passing of the Baton from Gen X to the Millenials." Strauss and Howe, in their recent book, *The Fourth Turning: An American Prophecy,* look at distinct patterns of human history and they document movements or "cycles" which last about the length of a long human life. These "cycles" are each composed of four turnings; a High (a period of confident expansion); an Awakening (a time of spiritual exploration and rebellion against established order); an Unraveling (an increasingly troubled era in which individualism triumphs over crumbling institutions); and a Crisis (a time when society passes through a great and perilous gate in history). Together the four turnings emulate history's seasonal rhythm of growth, maturation, entropy, and rebirth. Based on their observation of historical cycles the authors locate America as midway through an Unraveling; roughly a decade away from the next Crisis. The question for us is, "How have and will these 'turnings' affect youth culture?"

The youth that are currently entering young adulthood (Gen Xers) are into the third turning or the time of Unraveling. These are the kids born between 1961-1981.

They survived a hurried childhood of divorce, latchkeys, open classrooms, devil-child movies, and a shift from G to R ratings. They have heard themselves denounced as so wild and stupid as to put the nation at risk. They have had to maneuver through the sexual battlescape of aids. From grunge to "hip-hop" their splintery culture reveals a hardened edge. Their turning opened with a triumphant cheer that American individualism had arrived. But this individualism has drifted toward pessimism, growing violence, incivility, widening inequality, pervasive distrust of leaders and institutions, and debased popular culture. In common terms: Reality bites! Children raised worshiping the god of freedom and the American dream are spoiled and disillusioned kids. They are Nomads in a period of Unraveling.[2]

The Millennial kids, on the other hand, are the "Heros" born in 1982 and following.

They were born into a more child-friendly world when "baby on board" signs appeared in cars. As abortion and divorce rates ebbed, popular culture began stigmatizing hands off parenting styles and recasting babies as special. Hollywood is replacing child-devils with child-angels and politicians are defining adult issues in terms of effects on children. The increasing positivism and hands-on parenting is paying dividends as test scores continue to rise and a spirit of youthful cooperativism grows.[3]

Second, in a *Group Magazine* February '97 interview entitled "Invasion of the Millennials," William Strauss speaks about several positive turnings we will see taking place with the Millennial generation. First, optimism is combined with intense peer pressure, so peer pressure is seen as a solution rather than as a problem. Second, the motto for Gen Xers is "Just do it" whereas for Millennials it will be "Just do it together." Third, this generation will move from the negative, pessimistic disengagement to the belief that it can get things done. There is a general movement from negative labels and statistics to a sense of pride and accomplishment.[4]

Third, according to a recent *Christianity Today* study, further defining characteristics of Millennials include the following:

1. Born around 1980 . . . stepping into a world where Boomers revolution has been won and lost.
2. Pulse runs fast due largely to media bombardment . . . need frequent "hits."
3. Remote symbolizes reality . . . change is constant and focus is fragmented.
4. They've eaten from the tree of knowledge . . . they have a false sophistication (knowledge without wisdom).
5. Live for the now.
6. They are "jaded" having been there and done that attitude, nothing

---

[2]William Strauss and Neil Howe, *The Fourth Turning: An American Prophecy* (Broadway Books, 1997), 137.

[3]Ibid.

[4]Neil Howe, "Invasion of the Millenials," *Group Magazine* (February 1997).

shocks them. (Note: They have Dennis Rodman as a role model . . . they are the "Whatever" generation.)

7. Take consumerism for granted. ("Today's youth are shaped into consumers before they've had a chance to develop their souls," says David Denby.)

8. Cyber-suckled community . . . virtual reality safer place to be than real world. (Jim Taylor of Gateway 2000, one of the fastest growing computer manufacturers says, "By using the computer to find people who share your views, you can live in whatever kind of world you want. Reality is no longer a defined constant . . . it's a choice.")

9. Process info in narrative images.

10. B.S. detectors are always on.

11. Have had everything handed to them.

12. Don't trust adults . . . not anti-establishment of '60s, lack of trust is derived from the reality of societal breakdown, divorce, integrity breaches of leaders, heros, all of which have given legitimate reasons not to trust adults.[5]

Similarly, a Mennonite youth study concludes, "Today's teenagers look at life through the eyes that trust no one. Too many people have lied to them. Too many disappointments have happened. Too many people have let them down for them to simply give their trust away."[6]

What Kids Value Here are the top 10 things kids are saying, according to Ritch Hochstetler.

Tell the truth. When we talk to kids we need to talk about real life. We must admit that life is complicated, and that Jesus shows up in the midst of the complications.

God is present. Kids want to know how to hear the voice of God. They believe in God. We need to help them interpret what is being said.

Faith needs to count for something. Faith is dangerous. Thomas Merton has said, "If you tell God you want to become friends with the Holy Spirit be careful . . . he'll ask you to die."

Take me seriously. We must not be afraid to allow kids to try and fail in the church.

Speak a language kids can understand. There is a language problem: gender, exclusivity, etc. Don't take for granted that youth can understand terms and metaphors. Model family through relationships.

---

[5]Wendy Murray Zoba, "The Class of '00'," *Christianity Today* (February 1997): 20.

[6]Sara Bedsworth, "Mennonite Youth Today," Unpublished paper, May, 1997.

Speak a language of love and care.

Get real! Be authentic, honest, frank, and portray the real struggle of life. Don't overlook confusion and despair. Learn to listen; identify with pain. Theology and activities must embrace life. In a world of so much shallowness, kids expect the church to be real.

Be creative! Use imagery. How does the church convey the message of Christ? What image communicates best today in youth culture? Are we imaging Jesus of the gospel contextualized in our culture?

Be in relationship with me! Are we building bridges? Connect people to people, people to God, embrace plurality, foster a style of being religious with authenticity.

Lighten up! Don't lose your sense of humour. Connect with all people. Bonding is terribly important to ministry.

Be flexible! Don't be so bound to program. Be prepared to put square pegs in round holes.

Critical Concerns Based on my experience working with youth, here are some key concerns that we cannot ignore.

The busyness factor. Anyone working with youth today understands how incredibly busy kids are. They are in sports, working to support their lifestyle, trying to keep their heads above water in school, and often trying to survive in the context of a totally stressed out family.

> Teenagers today are too busy. There is so much for them to do with school work as well as with school activities. Many of them are holding down part-time jobs either to help out with money at home or to save up for those expensive Mennonite colleges.[7]

The greatest help we can provide is to give kids some source of stability. Be someone they can trust—someone who is not afraid to tell them the truth and say, "enough is enough!"

Positive yet fragile family environment. According to a recent study:

- Eighty-four percent lived with natural mother and father who were still married.
- Majority had good things to say about family as any person or group you love or care about deeply and who return the love and care to you.
- Sixty-two percent said they felt secure and loved.[8]

---

[7]Ibid.

[8]Josh McDowell, "Churched Youth Survey," 1994.

There is a lot of denial going on in Mennonite families. We have been acculturated by dominant North American society, even though we are reluctant to admit this. For example, studies tell us that sixty-five percent of Menno teens have lied to a parent, teacher, or older adult. Fifty-four percent have lied to one of their friends or peers. Bottom line: We don't have the time, have lost the effectiveness, and have compromised our integrity to communicate our faith and values to our children.

Hedonistic life orientation. Another study suggests that:

> The key cultural lesson we have to help children unlearn or combat with the truth of scripture is that the primary purpose of life is not pleasure. Kids and their families grow up seeking pleasure, avoiding pain, avoiding self discipline, avoiding any discomfort at all. We've got to give kids a realistic viewpoint of the struggle of life and work and self discipline; otherwise, they're always going to be disappointed or angry or frustrated if the think life should be fun all the time or easy.[9]

In the vernacular, "Our kids are spoiled!" They are products of our own creation. They have received too much too young and have an insatiable appetite for more. They have graduated from the school of materialism and have become "professional consumers."

"Waffling" personal sexual ethic. Menno kids tend to resort to situation ethics when it comes to premarital sex, even though overall statistics would tell us that they are sexually less active than the mainstream. Fear of pregnancy, discovery by parents, and peer pressure are determining factors according to the studies. Love for the person they think they might marry is a criterion for the decision to have sex.

Deep hunger for spirituality over religion. The following general characterizations of youth reflect current interests in spirituality over religion.

- They are seekers instead of joiners.
- They value eclectic teaching without concern for consistency.
- They search for what is deeply personal and spiritual over against keeping a list of rules.
- They emphasize that spirituality begins with an inner feeling or experience, not from a declaration of belief.

---

[9]Paul White quoted from *Children's Ministry Magazine* (November/December 1994).

- They value inner awareness over outward form and confining religiosity.

These observations point to the following general guideline which today's youth live by: follow your own bliss; your own needs. Youth have an overarching conviction that there is something more out there than this world has to offer.[10]

So what are the implications for the church? This is a time of opportunity. In a culture shaped by a personalistic world view that is yearning for truth to make some sense out of fragmented lives, the church has a message to share!

From a youth survey: "Eighty-two percent said they had made a personal commitment to Jesus Christ that was still important in their lives today. Yet, 49 percent said that no one can really prove which religion is absolutely true."[11]

"The conclusions from this survey suggest that the teenagers of today are struggling in their journey for truth. There is so much information coming at them from so many sources that they are striving to sort out what is truth."[12]

Engaging Mennonite students in "The Fourth Turning "

As we look to understand and relate with our Mennonite youth we must become students of history and youth culture. We must go beyond judgments based on outward appearances to focus on what our youth really believe and what they are most concerned about. Now is not the time to despair; rather, we stand at the doorway of opportunity. We have the opportunity to engage and challenge young people with the passion and relevance of life in Jesus Christ. But in order to do this, we must open our eyes to key signposts that will direct our path to connecting and reaching our kids. These should include the following:

We must begin by admitting our own arrogance. Leaders in the church often think they have the answer for our kid's questions. Henry Nouwen once said, "It takes a lot of humiliation for a little humility." What kids need is not our arrogance which communicates that we have the answer for all of life's questions, or "We have the package for you" but "We have the resources to help you live a meaningful life." What

---

[10]Lecture notes in "Princeton Forum on Youth Ministry," given by Wade Clark Roof, February 1997.

[11]Josh McDowell, "Churched Youth Survey," 1994.

[12]Sara Bedsworth, "Mennonite Youth Today."

is needed is a fresh approach; one that begins with people and there needs. This can come from bringing the resources of the church and the Christian tradition to the current needs of youth.

We must be clear about what it is we are trying to communicate. Values should be imparted, not only stated. Our values influence our world view, our behaviour, and our choices. "Values" can be described as a set of ethical beliefs or commitments that undergird how we interact with others and the world. Research has consistently found that young people's values have a great deal of influence on their behaviour. When young people hold positive values they are much more likely to make positive choices. Yet we rarely talk with young people about basic values such as honesty, caring, integrity, responsibility, equality, and self-control.

How can we teach values? The following have been suggested:

1. Be clear about our own! We need to nail down our priorities, beliefs, and commitments before we can teach them.

2. Model our values. Let kids see them in action.

3. Be consistent in what you say and do. (Unlike the youth pastor in Ohio who had an affair with a 15-year-old girl who was dating his son while he was leading other youth group kids in the True Love Waits campaign.)

4. Teach creatively . . . use stories, role plays, games.

5. Provide opportunities for kids to live values, i.e., kids learn responsibility by having responsibility.

6. Provide opportunities to reflect on values and experiences . . . give them a chance to talk about life experiences and ask tough questions.

7. Reinforce expressions of positive values . . . catch kids doing good! Acknowledge it and celebrate it!

8. Set boundaries that reflect and reinforce values . . . set rules and standards consistent with articulated values.

9. Teach social skills and competencies . . . nurture assertiveness, decision making, etc., so they know how to stand up for what you believe.

10. Involve youth in service, decision-making, and responsibility . . . let them practice and fail![13]

We must keep the faith that God is at work. What if the "Millennial Gen" is the next "Samuel Gen?" "What if they were entrusted by us to be keepers of the word? What would it take for this to become a reality? In Samuel's case it took a fat old teacher who came with the word of

---

[13]Peter L. Benson, *The Troubled Journey: A Profile of American Youth* (Washington, DC: Search Institute, 1996).

God repeatedly."[14]

We must never tire of coming to our youth, not only with information, but with an invitation to be in relationship with us and our Lord. We've got to focus on teaching the truth of the Bible within the context of relationships if we are going to reach this generation. We must be sensitive to the culture and language of our children in order to communicate the gospel with relevance and passion. Now is the time to act. It is a time of heightened spiritual searching in our society and in our world. We need to help youth discover a language, tradition, and story of faith that they can embrace with their hearts as well as their heads, in the context of relationship. We need to help them find their vocation and calling as something much larger than their occupation.

Conclusion Finally, in asking the question, "Who are Mennonite Youth?" we need to search our hearts as the Silent and Boomer generations and be open to reevaluate and reinvest our lives in the purposes of Christ and the privilege of ministry with our young people.

> Who is the typical American Mennonite Youth? Well, he/she is a person who is deeply confused and longing to know God in a personal way, but scared to give God total control of their life. The typical Mennonite teen of today is a scared little puppy looking for some arms to pick them up, explain life to them, and love them . . . . Are you up for the challenge?[15]

---

[14]Lecture notes from "Princeton Forum on Youth Ministry."

[15]Sara Bedsworth, "Mennonite Youth Today."

5 Teaching for Peace

Introduction Teaching for peace is a terribly important topic. I begin with two preliminary comments to underscore the importance. First, teaching for peace is important because I believe that there is steady and ongoing erosion of Mennonites' commitment to being a peace church. I fear that Mennonites are succumbing to temptations which make them less and less committed to actually being the peace church.

My malaise grows out of too many anecdotes and supposedly throwaway lines to be ignored. I am thinking of a letter-to-the-editor during the Gulf War of 1991 in which the writer stated, "I am a pacifist, but . . ." and then proceeded to use just war logic to rationalize both World War II and the Gulf War. Or a well-known Mennonite administrator who pointedly says in a public meeting, "I am just not as convinced as . . . that Mennonites need to be pacifists." Or the laments we frequently hear that "our peace stance makes evangelism more difficult." Or the statement by a widely recognized Mennonite pastor who said that mention of nonviolence should not appear in a General Conference fund-raising project in support of biblical principles because "we have talked enough about peace and pacifism, now we need to move on to other issues"—and his advice was obviously followed. Or the seeming desire to find ways to affirm common purpose with the military—whether in Somalia or Haiti or Bosnia-Herzegovina or in flood protection in Manitoba. Or the pastor who told me, "I know that you are right, but my people are tired of being different. They just want to blend in." Or an article by a Mennonite churchman who appeals

---

[1]Professor of Religion, Bluffton College.

to two-kingdom teaching as a rationalization for refusing to take a position on the Gulf War, when such a public declaration obviously supports the pro-war status quo. Or Mennonite academics who seem bent on arguing that the stories of violence-supporting personalities in Anabaptist history should make us willing to dialogue on the sword today. Or the action of the General Board of the Mennonite Church to save scarce budget dollars by eliminating support for Christian Peacemaker Teams and New Call to Peacemaking. While such comments and actions all have their individual and particular contexts and mitigating circumstances, they do not reassure me that our collective commitment to being a peace church continues strong.

To test our commitment is to ask what we are willing to pay for. Little more than a hundred years ago, Mennonites in Russia paid large amounts of money to fund the forestry service as alternative service for their young men of military age. In World War II, US Mennonites paid for Civilian Public Service (CPS). In volume four of the *Mennonite Experience in America* series, Paul Toews wrote that during World War II, Mennonite Central Committee spent $3,000,000 on CPS. In today's dollars, that is about $23,000,000. I fear our commitment is eroding. Would the Mennonite church today come up with $23,000,000 of new money for programs to keep its young people out of the military? It is true that more is involved than money. Toews also reported that church leaders feared that many Mennonite young men were unprepared to face the question of military service in World War II, and early in the war perhaps half of Mennonite young men entered the military, and a more complete study put the figure around 30 percent.[2] Figures are somewhat better today. Donald Kraybill and Leo Driedger report that 67 percent of General Conference young people and 80 percent of Mennonite Church young people would either accept alternative service or refuse draft registration altogether.[3]

The dollar discrepancy is still shocking, however, and clearly focuses the question of how deep the commitment is today to being a peace church. And there is a clear need for a major program to give Mennonite young people an alternative to the military. In the last couple of years, there has been growing pressure for Mennonite churches to

---

[2]Paul Toews, *Mennonites in American Society, 1930-1970: Modernity and the Persistence of Religious Community* (Scottdale, PA: Herald Press, 1996), 138, 148-149.

[3]*Mennonite Peacemaking: From Quietism to Activism* (Scottdale, PA: Herald Press, 1993), 166.

admit active duty military personnel as members. For our African American brothers, the military often appears as the only avenue to education, meaningful life, and escape from poverty. A letter-to-the-editor in the current *Gospel Herald* (10 June 1997) makes this point in a very poignant way. I wish that the Mennonite churches, which found $3,000,000 over a seven-year period to give their young men an alternative to World War II, would commit themselves to finding the equivalent $23,000,000 in the next seven years to provide meaningful job training and education for African American and other minority young men, who relate to the Mennonite churches.

That kind of interest and commitment will not happen without some very intentional teaching for peace. Teaching for peace is very important for the continuing persistence of Mennonites as a peace church. In his first address to the Bluffton College faculty, dean-elect John Kampen told us that our colleges were the key to the survival of the Mennonite churches. I believe that, and I believe that teaching for peace is vital to the survival of Mennonite churches as peace churches.

My second preliminary comment concerns the meaning of "peace." "Peace" is a popular term, and it covers a lot of territory. Everyone is for peace. "Peace" is often used to disguise war. We have "Peacekeeper" missiles. In the Gulf War, George Bush said, "We will be fighting for peace." After the Gulf War, I saw General Norman Schwarzkopf interviewed on Good Morning America, where the fawning host reached the inspired conclusion that Schwarzkopf was "a man of peace" because he expressed so much concern for his troops. Thus "peace" poses a temptation for the peace churches. Just as long as we keep peace general, we can blend into the North American mainstream. To avoid that temptation, when we talk about peace, I think that we should be as explicit as possible about what peace entails. When I talk about peace in this paper, I am talking about a multi-faceted package that would be unacceptable to the military leaders of our nations. Peace means proclaiming clearly that violence is wrong, and ought not to be rationalized. It means saying plainly that war is wrong, and that Christians ought not to participate. Peace means a principled pacifism, which declares that participation in war is never justified. Peace means a world view which considers Jesus' rejection of the sword intrinsic to his teaching, life and work, and thus war and violence can never be willingly rationalized or accepted by Christians.

The Curriculum It has been said that those of us gathered here represent a diverse group of institutions with widely varying curricula. There are Canadian and US contexts; university teaching centres and liberal arts colleges; both undergraduate and graduate programs. We have curricula for Bible and theology, for professional vocations and skilled trades, for science, the humanities and liberal arts. With all this diversity, one might wonder what these schools have in common.

I note at least two things in common. For one, these are all identified as *Mennonite* schools. And second, as a part of that identity, at some point in their curricula they all intend to teach *peace*.

With the diversity of missions displayed by these schools, the easy and tempting conclusion is that the church's teaching about peace has a bigger share of the curriculum for some schools than for others. For example, it would appear that a liberal arts college, whose comprehensive curriculum must cover a wide range of disciplines, might not be able to devote as much attention to peace as would a seminary, whose curriculum is confined to the religious disciplines and which offers a masters program in peace studies. That is an easy and perhaps frequent conclusion to reach. And I disagree with it. I want to tell you why I disagree.

There is one specific decision about peace that is common to each of our schools, regardless of our different curricula and differing institutional missions. I want to display that decision via some questions. You have probably discussed some form of these questions at each of your institutions. One question goes: "Is there a Mennonite, peace-church way to teach____?" Often the subject in the blank is something like chemistry or math or computer science, a subject where it appears that there is little correlation between Mennonite peace concerns and the subject, and that teaching the subject at a Mennonite school would not differ greatly from the way it was taught at a state university.

Another frequent question is, "Where does peace fit in the general education curriculum of a peace church college?" And the debate then concerns how much space—what percentage of hours taught—does peace get in the general education curriculum, and what other important material needs to be given up in order to make adequate room for peace.

Each of these ways of posing the question of peace in the curriculum assumes that there is some kind of a common core, some kind of an "education in general" and that peace is another element to be added into this education-in-general.

But for Mennonite schools, I would rather pose the question in another way. Is there "education-in-general," with the peace emphasis as an "add on"? Is a peace church education a standard core curriculum, with an additional course or series of courses which talk about peace? Or is all of education—whether specific disciplines or general education—shaped by assumptions of peace, nonviolence, and the rejection of violence? Is "peace" a component of the curriculum, lodged in a particular course or set of courses? Or is "peace" an assumption that shapes the entire curriculum and shapes the approach to every discipline?

This discussion about an education-in-general core is certainly not limited to Mennonite schools. It is going on all over. A rather well-known example appeared in the May 9 issue of *The Chronicle of Higher Education*. Stanford University instituted a new general education curriculum in 1988. This new curriculum was an effort to bridge the gap between two schools of thought about the existence of a core. One group argued that there is a standard core of classic documents—a kind of "Western canon"—that everyone ought to know about, even the science, pre-med and engineering students who make up 91 percent of the Stanford student body. This standard core is described as "the seminal works that have shaped humanist thought." At Stanford, this standard core, this education-in-general, would include names that are familiar to all of us—names like Socrates, Plato, Aristotle, the Bible, *The Iliad*, Dante, Shakespeare, John Stuart Mill, Thomas Paine, Jean-Jacques Rousseau, Thomas Jefferson, Karl Marx and Sigmund Freud. Those who advocate a general education curriculum that teaches these writers and documents believe strongly that they contain standard knowledge, an education-in-general, that is essential for understanding our basic western culture and values.

The other group says that since these materials were written almost exclusively by dead, white, mostly European males, a number of important perspectives are missing from this core. This revisionist faculty group believes that general education should also include writings that address issues of race, class, religion, and gender, and should include works by modern female and minority writers like Toni Morrison and Chinua Achebe. Proponents of the standard core talk about erosion of our common knowledge and common values and about the "death of the Western canon" when some classic components have been cut in order to clear space and time for the more recent "special interests" represented by Morrison and Achebe. The innovators reply that it is perspective more than specific documents that is important—the important thing is to teach students that the world looks differently when seen through the eyes of women or Africans or Native Americans or African Americans, and it is more important to teach students to see through new eyes than it is to put them in contact with specific pieces of classic literature.

Where do the Mennonite peace church colleges fit into this kind of debate? I believe very strongly that peace church colleges must do more than teach the standard, western canon. Right alongside the discussion about the need for perspectives other than those of dead, white males, Mennonite peace church colleges should be clambering to say that a nonviolent perspective and interpretation of the core is missing. Mennonite colleges should be teaching students what the world looks like through nonviolent eyes, and that that nonviolent perspective frequently overlaps with and reinforces the critique of the classic core made by feminists and Native American and African American writers.

Posing the Mennonite discussion in conversation with the Stanford discussion also points to a second question. That question concerns the content of the core. Hearing the description of Stanford's core ought to bring us to realize that simply making the assumption that there is a standard core, an education-in-general, does not produce agreement on what belongs in that core. I would hope that Mennonite colleges want to include some items in the core that Stanford does not consider important, and that we would probably omit some which they consider important.

An additional component of the discussion of the content of the core is the fact that our knowledge is growing rapidly. As a variety of jokes point out, children today have a more difficult time in history than their grandparents did because there is a lot more history now. And there is almost exponential growth of knowledge in science and technology, and that technology in turn has provoked new kinds of studies and growth in knowledge in many other disciplines. This growth in knowledge means that there is increased competition among disciplines for space in the core, and it is an additional reason why general education ought not be to defined by any version of the traditional classic standard core.

But we do not need to debate the question today about what goes into the core. The more important point that I want to make is that whatever goes into that core, the rejection of violence that we learn from the reign of God must be integral to the interpretation of whatever ends up in the core. And beyond any discussion of a core, the peace stance of the Mennonite churches, the rejection of violence learned from the reign of God, should shape our approach to education across the entire range of disciplines that we teach.

I have a few examples, scattered across the disciplines, to illustrate how a nonviolent world view should be present and visible throughout our educational endeavour. These examples are not definitive statements. At every step of the way there will be specialists who know much more about each subject or discipline than I do. I present these comments as discussion starters. They are indications of the kind of issues we will face if we seriously believe that violence and war are wrong and that Jesus' rejection of the sword reflects the rule of the reign of God and is thus a shaping norm for people who identify with Jesus Christ.

Teaching history. The peace church teaching of history is not just teaching the history of the peace churches and the history of pacifism. It should involve a nonviolent perspective on the history that everyone else teaches about.

i) The treatment of the European discovery of North America. When I was in grade school, I learned what a smart and courageous hero Columbus was to discover America, and about the ignorant people who lived here but did not know what to do with the land, and fortunately the Europeans came along to settle the barren wilderness. We are now starting to recognize some of the cruel and brutal acts committed by Columbus and most of the European explorers, and school texts are now recognizing and saying some kind things about Native Americans and Native American culture. The new line is to recognize both the good and the bad in the conduct of Columbus and in the settlement of North America. I guess that is a gain over the earlier version of heroic Europeans conquering savage Indians and a barren continent—but not much of a gain.

Teaching us to accept the "good and bad" is just a more sophisticated way to accommodate violence against the first inhabitants of the land. Accepting the "good and the bad" is still just a rationalization of violence. It is a claim that good can result from violence, and that it was necessary to sacrifice the first nations for the larger good, the good of the Europeans. History teaching at a peace church college should challenge this violence-accommodating view of the settlement of North America by Europeans.

ii) The war of 1776. Children in US schools are taught repeatedly that war is good, that war brings freedom, that war and freedom are linked. That teaching begins with their first lesson about the founding of the nation in 1776. Supposedly "we" are free because of that war. Or take the US Civil War. Our children are taught that without war, the slaves could not have been freed. James Juhnke, history professor at Bethel College, is currently at work, co-authoring a history of the United States which challenges those assumptions about the goodness of war. The book will show that there were always alternatives to war, and that war is really the result of a failure of imagination. When one begins to see the alternatives, it becomes obvious that war is not inevitable. In fact war is a learned activity and a specifically chosen activity.

The Canadians all know the falsity of these United States claims. By what is taught to US school children, namely that there cannot be freedom without war, Canada is still an oppressed country. We in the United States need Canadians to remind us to challenge the view of history taught in all public schools in the United States, and to provide a fundamental critique of United States history.

iii) Teaching Anabaptist history. The last 25 years of Anabaptist historiography have shown quite clearly and convincingly that the sixteenth-century Anabaptist movements were not the uniformly pacifist groups that Harold S. Bender's *Anabaptist Vision* portrayed. The big question is what we will do with that data. I am increasingly disturbed at the number of Mennonite historians who are saying that this violent Anabaptist history teaches us to dialogue on the sword. Or that the violent component of our history should help us to be more understanding and open to the question of military Mennonites today. Our history need not teach us such things unless we choose an interpretation that accommodates violence. Interpreting Anabaptist history is not different than interpreting American history: do we fall in to the violence-accommodating mode of North America, and begin to interpret the violent acts in our story as events that prepare us today to incorporate military Mennonites? *Or*, do we interpret the violent episodes of our story as instances of failure and lack of imagination and as tragic deviations in the process of becoming a more faithful church?

Teaching a nonviolent world view. Following upon the discussion of North American history, *education* as a discipline ought to be strongly and clearly shaped by a nonviolent world view. A peace church college should do more than make sure that teachers are kind to children and can mediate playground fights. It should do more than make sure each new teacher has the facts to meet state certification requirements. As I said, one of the purposes of public school education in the United States is to teach our children that war and freedom are linked. We need to develop new elementary and secondary education curricula. When new teachers leave a peace church college, they should have in their hands an alternative curriculum, which teaches the injustice of North American settlement and that wars are mistakes rather than the basis for "freedom and democracy." And peace church colleges should give students strategies for using that curriculum as much as possible in their teaching careers without getting fired by patriotic school boards.

Teaching criminal justice. Should we develop programs which teach people to work gently within the system, making sure guards and police officers are kind and sensitive people? I suggest that teaching for peace means teaching to expose the vengeance-oriented, retribution-driven character of our judicial systems, and to pose a specific alternative to it: something like Victim Offender Reconciliation Programs.

Teaching psychology and sociology. Our commitment to nonviolence should make us sensitive to numerous specific issues in the disciplines of psychology and sociology. Some of these specific issues concern direct violence, such as child abuse, spouse abuse, sexual abuse, abortion or capital punishment. Other concerns reflect issues of structural violence—poverty caused by public policy or the systemic racism that is a factor in both the United States and Canada.

However, beyond these specific discussions, working from a nonviolent perspective can have an impact on the disciplines themselves. These disciplines make assumptions about what is "normal" when it comes to aggression and violence as inherent characteristics of humanity. Or they make assumptions about the kind of changes and transformations that people can make, either by their own efforts or with the help of God under the influence of what theologians call "grace." Are human beings innately and inevitably inclined to violence? And if so, is acting on those inclinations inevitable and justified? And if it is innate, can those inclinations be modified, overcome, transformed? Or rather, is violent behaviour something that is learned? If violence is learned, can it be unlearned?

Our answers to such questions depend, to some extent, on whether our approach to the disciplines of psychology and sociology, our framing of the questions and our search for answers, is shaped by assumptions derived from a nonviolent, peace church world view, or from a world view which accommodates violence as natural and inevitable. And on the question about the inevitability of violence, particularly of war, remember the learnings from the study of history, namely that war is not inevitable at all—it is very much a learned and chosen activity.

Teaching science. Science is not neutral; it is not a disembodied cultureless and valueless entity. It does accept unquestioned givens—assumptions—that reflect a larger world picture. Even if the relationship between science and a nonviolent world view is less immediate than in some other disciplines, I want to make a few comments about science, theology, and nonviolence.

i) We must distinguish between science and ultimate statements, or between science and theology. Science paints a picture of the physical dimension of reality; it describes how things work in the physical realm. But science has its limits.

It is *not* a statement about God, or a statement about ultimate reality per se. We need to be clear that not "seeing" God in the laboratory is not a statement about God's non-existence.

Theology does talk about ultimate reality and the meaning of our existence if one starts with the assumption that God exists. But, like science, theology also has its limits. Theology consists of the words we use to construct our ideas about God for worship and meaning. Theology should not claim that these words depict God directly or univocally. And theology should *not* attempt to describe *how* things work in the physical realm.

ii) This means that evolution *cannot* be in conflict with good theology. If science says that some version of evolution is the best explanation for how things work in the physical realm—the non-ultimate realm—then evolution is true in that realm, and theology has no business denying it. But in the same way, describing some kind of evolutionary development in the physical realm is not a statement about ultimate reality; it is not a statement about "God," who in some way is the origin of the process or the "serendipitous creativity" which guides the process.

iii) But even when science should limit its description of reality to the physical realm, it is important to recognize that science does plug into a value-laden world view. Those values can show up at what appear to be more mundane levels—mundane with respect to the big issues of the relationship of science and theology.

Values show up in the way science faculty guide students in the choice of careers in science. Values show up in the kind of examples that faculty use in the classroom to illustrate scientific material and scientific findings—ecological impact versus industrial applications; vectors and trajectories that do not involve bullets, rockets, and military imagery. Possibilities are limited only by our imaginations.

While the relationship between science and a nonviolent world view is less immediate than for some other disciplines, making nonviolence visible in the assumptions and values that one brings to the teaching of science is an important part of what it means to be a scientist at a peace church college.

Teaching mathematics. For mathematics, my comments resemble those for science. Faculty communicate a nonviolent world view and peace church values in how they counsel students about careers in math and applications of mathematics. There are also some very real nonviolent, peace church lessons that one can teach via mathematics, and in the math problems students are asked to solve. For example, have students calculate how many or how much of various kinds of good things the US could have purchased for Iraq with money spent per missile, per missile attack, and for the entire Gulf War to destroy Iraq. While students calculate, they can reflect on whether giving some of that stuff to Iraq might have had more impact on changing Iraq's attitudes and conduct than killing its citizens and destroying its infrastructure. Or after the Civil War, the suggestion was laughed at that freed African slaves should receive 40 acres and a mule as a compensation for slavery and a start toward a free life. There was no land to give away, it was said. Well, have students in a math class calculate how many slaves could have received 40 acres if the land given free to wealthy white guys to build railroads had been given to penniless slaves. And then calculate the loss to the economy by keeping the freed slaves in poverty rather than allowing them to become productive. The use of such examples in math is bounded only by our imaginations and the time needed to develop them. And while students are working on such a problem, they can reflect on the fact that whoever received the free land, it was stolen from Native Americans.

Teaching economics. Economic systems can camouflage a great deal of systemic violence. The economic theory of Neo-liberalism uses the language of freedom and the gospel of private ownership. It sounds good. But it is really a rationalization for the concentration of wealth in fewer and fewer hands at the expense of the poor in third world countries. Students of economics at a peace church college should learn about the systemic violence of free market theories like neo-liberalism.

Teaching physical education, and coaching. Nonviolence should shape how we view competitive sports.

Not infrequently, people who profess nonviolence have doubts about competitive sports. Competition seems violent. Football seems violent. I watched a lot of the Stanley Cup playoffs on TV, and one can obviously raise violence questions about hockey.

However, I do not think that competition is inherently violent. Nonviolence should shape our attitude toward competition—but not simply to object to competition or even to contact. The real question concerns how the players view the game and the opponent. Is a competitive game a substitute for "war," in which the object is to humiliate and destroy the opponent, mentally and even physically? I think not. I suggest that competitive sport is really a cooperative endeavour, in which each player and each side actually needs the other and is in fact helping the other to find his or her limits or to reach heights not previously attained. And the understanding that competitive sports are a cooperative endeavour, which is a learning shaped in part by a nonviolent world view, should have a profound impact on the way coaches prepare a team, as well as on the way players conduct themselves in a game.

I can add that an understanding of nonviolence has given me a different understanding of the so-called "killer instinct." I think that it is really the capacity to shut out distractions and to focus on the problem at hand—and it is the same kind of concentration that musicians want to have when they play for a crowd, or that a minister might draw on when called suddenly to speak in a highly exposed setting. We ought not allow that kind of concentration to be identified as inherently violent by the phrase "killer instinct," which comes to us with favourable connotations from a world that lauds redemptive violence.

Teaching art, literature, music. Nonviolence is a perspective from which to examine the arts throughout human history. A number of years ago, one of my colleagues procured a Bluffton College summer research grant to study the artistic depictions of war and peace throughout western religious history. Her findings were rather shocking—western art glorifies war, and there was virtually *no peace art* until the anti-war art of the Vietnam War era. Such an observation constitutes a rather frightening indictment of western civilization via art history.

Another colleague is currently engaged in an analysis of medieval chivalric writing and the formation of King Arthur's Round Table as a military force sworn to maintain peace and uphold justice. Working from a principled nonviolent perspective, her analysis shows that what is frequently depicted as a gentlemanly tradition to limit war and conflict is actually just another set of language for applying justifiable war arguments, and that the effort to control violence by more violence ultimately fails.

Teaching theology. The western Christian theological tradition has accommodated violence. It has not ruled pacifism and nonviolence to be heretical, the way it ruled out views of Pelagius or Arius or Apollinarius. But the western, classic theological tradition has accommodated the sword and it has made rejection of the sword a peripheral matter. Until the last few years, Mennonites have espoused the theology that accommodates violence, except that Mennonites added nonresistance and pacifism to that violence-accommodating package. And we have maintained rejection of just war and pacifism as the official stance of the denomination. For the most part, our strong ecclesiology, reinforced by a rather strong ethnic identity, has reminded us to keep nonviolence and the rejection of the sword as add-ons to the violence-accommodating theology of western Christendom.

One part of this picture is changing. Our ethnic identity is fast fading. And in any case, we need something better than ethnic glue to preserve the tradition of nonviolence that is integral to Jesus' story. If Mennonites want to continue to be a peace church, we need to develop a better theology than we have been borrowing from the Christendom tradition that accommodated war. If we genuinely believe that Jesus' rejection of the sword is intrinsic to who he was and to what he did, that better theology will pose an alternative to the theology of Christendom. In this better theology, Jesus' rejection of violence will appear in Christology and atonement in ways which make unavoidably clear that accommodation of war and violence is quite incompatible with the reign of God made visible in Jesus.

How willing we are to develop such a theology is, I would argue, a faith statement about whether nonviolence really is linked to the life and the work of Jesus. Starting with Christendom's theology is already to declare rejection of the sword peripheral to the good news about Jesus. I call on the Mennonite churches to have the courage to work on and accept a theology which makes rejection of the sword a central insight, rather than allowing a desire for ecumenical openness to lull us into accepting Christendom's core theology which has accommodated violence. Our future continuance as a peace church depends on it. If Christendom's core really was the foundation of peace theology, as some of our theologians are claiming, then all those adherents of Christendom's orthodoxy out there would already be pacifists.

Conclusion I have not treated peace and nonviolence as add-ons to someone else's assumed standard core or education-in-general. The idea of a standard core, with an added section for "peace" is how many liberal arts curricula deal with "peace," if it is dealt with at all. Such an approach accepts the violence-accommodating world view and ethos as a given, and does not mount a fundamental challenge to it. In contrast, my intent was to sketch ways that nonviolence is an integral dimension of the study of a variety of disciplines.

Peace church education ought not be education-in-general, with the peace church contribution being merely to propose one further item to add at some point in an assumed standard outline. Our discussions ought not to be an argument about which piece of the standard curriculum or education-in-general we have to give up in order to make room for peace.

Rather I think that peace church education ought to feature a curriculum that top to bottom is shaped by the belief that nonviolence and the rejection of the sword is central to the reign of God, and an integral dimension of the life and teaching of Jesus Christ who makes that reign visible.

I have been talking about a subject that Mennonites ought to agree with, if they are a peace church. However, I want to make it very explicit that I have not been talking about an approach to education that only long time Mennonites can comprehend. I have hardly referred to "Mennonite" at all. And in fact, some of the people committed most strongly to nonviolence among my faculty colleagues are people who did not grow up Mennonites, but who were attracted to the Mennonite churches or a Mennonite college *because* of its peace tradition. Rather than pushing "Mennonite," I have talked about how an assumption of nonviolence can shape our approach to academic issues. And that discussion is in no way limited to people who grew up in the Mennonite tradition.

In fact, it is not even necessary to change traditions in order to understand or accept it. What is required is that one perceive and understand that rejection of violence is intrinsic to the story of Jesus and to the *Christ*ian gospel—and then that one begin to apply that gospel to other issues.

In fact, wherever one is lodged in terms of membership, the question of violence cannot be avoided. There will always be a decision whether to look at the world from the violence-accommodating perspective of the North American ethos, or from the perspective of the violence-rejecting narrative of the peace church understanding of Jesus. Most North American Christians make the decision about violence by default—they just accept the violence-accommodating world view without reflection. And not to decide, and just to go with the flow, is really to vote with the violence-accommodating status quo. My challenge to the would-be peace church is very consciously and specifically to make the choice to believe that Jesus means nonviolence, and then to look at our entire educational endeavour from that perspective. The continuation of Mennonites as a peace church depends on it.

----

6 *Encomium Pietatis*: Teaching for Community

Dale Schrag[1]

Introduction I have always called him "Butch." His given name is Joseph; surname Goering. I learned to know him while I was in high school. Though we attended different schools, we became fast, and lasting, friends. I went to Bethel College; he ventured off to the University of Kansas. There he discovered John Milton and Thomas Aquinas (and Paula), and he would never be the same. His graduate school career began at Yale Divinity School on a Rockefeller Fellowship, and ended at the Pontifical Institute for Medieval Studies at the University of Toronto, where Butch earned his Ph.D. in medieval studies. He has been at Toronto ever since. His first appointment was in the department of history; currently he chairs the department for the study of religion at the University of Toronto.

Speaking of religion, Butch came from Mennonite stock (mother, Mennonite Brethren; father, General Conference), but Butch was raised Evangelical United Brethren (EUB). (His father had a falling out with the Mennonites, at least in part over participation in World War II.) His wonderful wife Paula, whom he met at Kansas University, is Jewish. Today Butch himself is a practicing Roman Catholic.

So why would I begin a presentation on "teaching for community" at a conference on Mennonite Higher Education by talking about a Roman Catholic professor at the University of Toronto? Some of you, I'm sure, are wondering. And some of you, I suspect, think you have the answer. Here, after all, is the case for Mennonite education in a nutshell. He who goes to a Mennonite college ends up marrying a

---

[1]Director of Marketing and Church Relations and General Conference Secretary for Higher Education.

Mennonite woman and working in a Mennonite institution; he who goes off to the secular university marries a Jewish woman and ends up, not only working at a secular institution, but converting to Catholicism!

Your conclusion may be valid, but that it is not why I told you about Butch. I chose to begin this presentation with Butch Goering because I have learned—and continue to learn—so very much from him, about education and even about community. I have learned from him, for example, the importance of holding the discipline at arm's length. Here is a man who is undeniably erudite. He has published numerous books and scholarly articles, books with titles like, Templum Dei *of Robert Grosseteste* and *William de Montibus: the Schools and the Literature of Pastoral Care*, books from presses like the Pontifical Institute for Medieval Studies at the University of Toronto, books of 650 pages with price tags like $95.00 per volume. But to hear him tell it, Butch takes relatively little pride in that record of scholarly production. "It's what one has to do," he says, "in order to teach." And teaching is, for Butch, decidedly *not* an exercise in Ph.D. creation. Rather, it's an opportunity to engage students in a serious and meaningful dialogue with the past, an opportunity for them to discover for themselves that the questions with which they struggle today are questions with which human beings throughout history have struggled. I doubt that Butch would care one whit if he never generated a single graduate student from his undergraduate teaching; that's not why he teaches. He teaches, I think, because he wants to use history as a means of forming character, of cultivating virtue, of helping men and women become better persons.

Last Christmas Butch visited me during his break. He told me he was about to become chair of the department for the study of religion at the University of Toronto. "What," he asked me, "is your impression of religious studies?" "As a discipline?" I countered. I began speaking in general terms about the academic world's view of religious studies, and, as I recall, I came up with a description much like that of Robert Proctor in his stimulating book, *Education's Great Amnesia*. Proctor writes,

> . . . the academic study and teaching of religion has moved away from theology and metaphysics, and has adopted instead the disciplines of anthropology, sociology, and psychology to describe and explain the experience of the sacred. Since their methodological perspectives require that they explain whatever phenomenon they may be studying as a human construct, these disciplines are incapable of considering the existence of anything which transcends the human. When they meet the belief in the divine, they reduce it to the product of social, cultural, psychological

factors.[2]

Proctor may overstate the case a bit here, but as I recall, so did I. Butch listened intently, and then nodded his agreement. "I think that's a pretty accurate assessment," he said. The twinkle in his eye demanded a response from me. "So what's *your* view of religious studies?" I obliged. "As chair of the department for the study of religion at the University of Toronto," he answered, "I will have one overriding objective for my department, and that will be to promote piety in our students."

It was, to say the least, not the answer that I expected (nor, I'll venture to guess, the answer *you* expected). But I'd like to suggest this morning, at least for purposes of discussion, that it may provide an important key to teaching for community. Indeed, I will attempt to argue that the most effective and lasting "teaching for community" begins with a prior step—teaching for piety. Thus I have titled this presentation, "*Encomium pietatis* ("In Praise of Piety"): Teaching for Community." My use of the Latin title is not, I hope, an exercise in academic arrogance and superciliousness, but rather an effort to express the fact that Butch's call to teach for piety is not a new position, but a very, very old one, one that has recurred again and again throughout history. One of those times, in fact, was during a period of special interest to Mennonites, the early sixteenth century.

The Crisis of Community But now we're getting ahead of ourselves. Before we try to make the case for teaching for piety as a way to teach for community, it may be appropriate to acknowledge the crisis of community in contemporary North America. I suspect we need not spend much time here; I assume I am preaching to the choir. We've all read *Habits of the Heart*.[3] We know that the spectre of individualism is gnawing away at any semblance of community in our neighbourhoods—perhaps in our churches, and even families, as well. Cheryl Russell is a demographer who has spent much of her professional career examining, surveying, testing Baby Boomers and their children. In 1993 she published *The Master Trend: How the Baby Boom Generation Is Remaking America* (Plenum Press). The "master

---

[2]Robert E. Proctor, *Education's Great Amnesia: Reconsidering the Humanities from Petrarch to Freud, with a Curriculum for Today's Students* (Bloomington, IN: Indiana University Press, 1988), 167.

[3]Robert N. Bellah, et.al., *Habits of the Heart: Individualism and Commitment in American Life* (New York: Harper and Row, 1985).

trend" she identifies is rampant, pervasive individualism. She minces no words:

> The master trend of individualism drives a myriad of smaller trends. *It* is behind the rise in divorce and violent crime. *It* is the reason for soaring health-care costs, political gridlock, and racial tensions . . . . Individualists put their personal needs ahead of community needs. They make commitments for personal gain rather than for moral reasons . . . . today's and tomorrow's young adults are bound to be even more individualistic than baby boomers. They will also be more materialistic, more career-oriented, and less trusting of others.[4]

If Russell is right, we clearly have a problem, and it's going to get worse before it gets better. It would appear that *all* colleges and universities ought to be concerned about, and seek to counteract, this trend, but for any such institutions who claim to be grounded in the Anabaptist-Mennonite ethos, it ought to be of special import. For over 450 years we have claimed "community" to be a defining characteristic of what it means to be Anabaptist-Mennonite, though I suspect there's been a great deal of "slippage" on this issue in the Mennonite church. In general, we don't think "corporately" any more; we measure most things—including our church commitments—almost entirely on how it affects us (or perhaps our immediate family). And if the church isn't "meeting my needs" sufficiently, then, in the words of the old song, "you'd better shop around!"

This individualism undoubtedly derives from a veritable host of causes and conditions, but I would like to lift out two themes for your consideration. The first I term "the catechism of 'No Fear.'" In his stimulating book, *Moral Fragments and Moral Community; A Proposal for Church in Society*, Larry Rasmussen introduces the concept of "catechisms . . . which impart elementary wisdom, the kind we use time and again as rudder and guide."[5] If the primary catechism is popular culture (and I think that for all too many of our students it is), we need not ponder long why individualism is everywhere ascendant and community is everywhere in decline. Consider the catechism of "No Fear." You've seen the tee shirts; you've seen the logo on the back of pick-up trucks. It's a stroke of marketing genius. It focuses on a climate of "take-no-prisoners, in-your-face" arrogance that

---

[4]Cheryl Russell, "The Master Trend," *American Demographics* 15 (October 1993): 30, 36-37.

[5](Minneapolis: Fortress Press, 1993), 88.

infuses professional, now college, sometimes even high school athletics *and* big business. The perfect combination.

The ancient Greeks had a saying: "Where there is fear there is modesty."[6] Consider the contrapositive of that one. Is the fact that we live in a society characterized by immodesty, impudence, insolence, arrogance, perhaps a consequence of a catechism of "no fear"? Meaningful community, of course, demands all of the opposite characteristics: civility, humility, good manners. And lasting community, I would argue, demands another kind of fear: the fear of the Lord. In the 1960s, "intentional communities" were springing up all over this country. With very few (if any) exceptions, the only ones that endured had a clearly-defined religious focus. I can think of two reasons why this might be the case. First, focus on the divine allows us to get beyond the particularities of pluralism and find a truly common commitment. Second, the human propensity to sin is too strong (especially when we are bombarded by a prevailing culture that suggests that the exalted individual need answer to no one); even when the spirit is willing, the flesh is weak. We need help from outside of ourselves; we need transcendence; we need to fear and worship the Transcendent One.

In addition to the catechism of "No Fear," I offer a second contributor to the crisis of community: the death of the past. I have borrowed the phrase from J. H. Plumb in his book of the same title. Plumb argues that our sense of discontinuity with the ages that preceded us derives in no small part from our reliance on technology.[7] I don't disagree, but it should be noted that 150 years earlier, in a much less technologically-driven age, Alexis de Tocqueville made a similar prediction: "The woof of time is every instant broken and the track of generations effaced. Those who went before are soon forgotten; of those who will come after, no one has any idea: the interest of man is confined to those in close propinquity to himself."[8] Whether the result of advancing technology or a development intrinsic to democracy, the reality, says Christopher Lasch, is that "To live for the moment is the

---

[6]Desiderius Erasmus, *Adages: Ii1 to Iv100*, vol. 31 of *Collected Works of Erasmus* (Toronto: University of Toronto Press, 1982), 207.

[7]J. H. Plumb, *The Death of the Past* (Boston: Houghton Mifflin Company, 1970), 14-15. There is, incidentally, much more to Plumb's argument than the impact of technology.

[8]*Democracy in America*, 2 vols. (New York: Vintage Books, 1954), vol. 2: 105.

prevailing passion—to live for yourself, not for your predecessors or posterity. We are fast losing the sense of historical continuity, the sense of belonging to a succession of generations originating in the past and stretching into the future."[9] Robert Proctor blames the death of the past for our "pathological narcissism,"[10] and our inability to describe a morality that transcends individual self-interest.[11] The "death of the past," or, put another way, the "cult of contemporaneity" reinforces at every turn the concept of the autonomous self, beholden to no one.

Little wonder, then, that we are experiencing a crisis of community. Community demands a common agenda, common commitments, a common story. It is nurtured by rituals and symbols that re-tell that story, reinforce those commitments, renew that agenda. Individualism resists the common agenda and commitments; pluralism seems to preclude the common story (in any case, the cult of contemporaneity would ensure that the story is a short one), and the prevailing secularism prohibits relying on a transcendent focus for the common commitment; finally, cynicism (another hallmark of modernity—or postmodernity) scoffs at the rituals and symbols.

The Power of Piety Does piety offer a meaningful antidote to the virulence of individualism? Is it a necessary antecedent to real community? First, what do I mean by "piety"? Let me begin by suggesting what "piety" is not. Some years ago I was teaching Anabaptist history to a high school Sunday school class. For our first session, I asked them if they perceived any substantive differences between the Mennonite students at Newton High School and those students who were not Mennonite. (Their answer, predictably, was "not much.") Then I shared with them some quotations from H. S. Bender's "The Anabaptist Vision" speech; quotations from the *enemies* of the Anabaptists like Ulrich Zwingli, Heinrich Bullinger, Franz Agricola, etc., all of whom admitted that the lives of the Anabaptists were striking in their "blamelessness." Many of these quotations used the word "piety" or "pious" in their description of the Anabaptists. When I was done, I smugly asked the students what they thought. I expected answers that would reveal a new-found reverence for their Anabaptist forebears. Instead, the very first response was, "Why would anyone want to be considered pious?"

---

[9]*The Culture of Narcissism: American Life in an Age of Diminishing Expectations* (New York: W. W. Norton, 1978), 5.

[10]Proctor, 163.

[11]Ibid., 174.

When I use the term "piety" today, it does *not* mean, as I think it did for this high school student, "sanctimony" or "self-righteousness." It is not even directly related to "pietism" (though I would also argue that we educated Mennonites are too paranoid about pietism, but that's a topic for another sermon). Pietism has a much more "emotional" essence than does piety, at least in the sense that I am using the latter term. For I am using "*pietas*" (piety) in its classical and Renaissance sense, and in that context the essence of piety is focused on moral and ethical behaviour. A few examples.

For the Romans, *pietas* or "piety" involved "dutiful respect" toward the gods, the motherland, parents and other relatives. For the Greek view of piety, I begin, and end, with Socrates. "Socrates . . . believed that piety requires that a man engage in the craft of just service to the god." [Notice that "god" is singular for Socrates.] Of what did that "service" consist? Socrates was convinced that "what god wanted most for men [was] the abandonment of their pretence of wisdom and the comprehension that their material concerns profit them nothing until they have first achieved that most precious good, human virtue."[12]

In that rediscovery of classical civilization that so characterized the Renaissance, these classical notions of piety did not go unnoticed. Desiderius Erasmus, prince of the sixteenth-century humanists, and a man who profoundly influenced many (probably most) of our Anabaptist forebears, sought to preserve a connection between classical understandings of piety (what Erasmus termed "natural piety") and "Christian piety." He argued that the former was "pre-Christian, not sub-Christian." In fact, in his colloquy *The Godly Feast*, Erasmus scandalized Martin Luther by making a reference to "Saint Socrates."[13] "Natural piety," for Erasmus, "signifies 'all affection, worship, and dutiful action which we owe to those from whom we have received life' . . . . It is the innate disposition of reverence toward all life-givers, first

---

[12]Nicholas Smith and Thomas Brickhouse, "The Origin of Socrates' Mission," *Journal of the History of Ideas* 44 (October-December 1983): 666. This represents a somewhat unique interpretation. In the Platonic dialogue *Euthyphro*, Socrates sought an answer to the question "What is piety?" Most scholars would argue that the question goes unanswered in that dialogue, but Smith and Brickhouse have suggested that a clearer sense of Socrates' understanding of piety can be had by considering his *Apology* before the Athenian Senate in light of his comments in the *Euthyphro*. I find their argument a compelling one.

[13]Desiderius Erasmus, *The Colloquies of Erasmus*, translated by Craig R. Thompson (Chicago: University of Chicago Press, 1965), 68.

of all God."[14] "Christian piety," for Erasmus, is, in its essence, the imitation of Christ, "the only complete example of perfect piety."[15] (An idea, I think, that bears a striking resemblance to the Anabaptist understanding of discipleship.) "Perfect piety," wrote Erasmus, ". . . joins us together with God . . . so that we are made one with him."[16]

This, then, is "piety" for the purposes of this paper: at its most basic level, an attitude of dutiful respect for the past; at its most profound level, the effort to be "joined together with God" through the imitation of Christ. The moral-ethical demands of piety are clear and consistent, from the most basic level to the most profound. Though the latter piety requires deep faith and belief (hence "pietism" is not totally irrelevant here), the test of that fait—in typical Anabaptist fashion—is in the resulting behaviour.

How would this type of piety counteract the catechism of "No Fear" and the "cult of contemporaneity"? Let's begin with the latter. This idea that the newest is the truest is a position of enormous arrogance. One of piety's great gifts to us would be to dissuade us of such a notion. Paul Oskar Kristeller, perhaps the greatest scholar of Renaissance humanism in the twentieth century, attempts to do precisely that with his call for respecting, yea *treasuring,* the past. "In the long run," says Kristeller, "it is not the past that is measured by us, but we ourselves will be measured by it and judged by it, since we have to prove to the future that we have lived up to the standards of the past."[17] That is

---

[14]Erasmus, quoted in Manfred Hoffmann, "Faith and Piety in Erasmus's Thought," *The Sixteenth Century Journal* 20 (Summer 1989): 255.

[15]Erasmus, quoted in Richard L. DeMolen, *The Spirituality of Erasmus* (Nieuwkoop: De Graaf Publishers, 1987), 51.

[16]Hoffman, 256.

[17]"The Unity of Truth," in *Renaissance Thought and Its Sources* (New York: Columbia University Press, 1979), 210. Kristeller is not naive. He does not assume that everything in the past is worth preserving. He says: "We should neither uncritically admire nor imitate the past but neither can we afford to completely ignore it. We must know it first before we can take from it what we can use and approve, while rejecting the rest . . . . Human civilization is a cumulative process, and any part of it is more easily and more quickly destroyed than rebuilt. No single generation can hope to build or rebuild it from the bottom, and hence we should gratefully accept and appreciate the building materials which past periods no less creative than ours have left to us. It is an inheritance each generation is called upon to hand on to its successor. It cannot help ignoring or destroying a part of this heritage, but it should always try to preserve what is worth preserving and to add something better

natural piety at its best, and that, I submit, is an appropriate recipe for walking gently and intelligently into the future. Even a moment's reflection reveals that this natural piety, at its core, is anti-individualistic. By showing reverence to and for all those external factors that have shaped one's character, one is "protected," as it were, from the sin of self-centredness. And the catechism of "No Fear," a catechism predicated on arrogance and insolence, would surely melt away when fully exposed to the light of Christian piety, modeled after the self-sacrificial love of Jesus Christ.

Education as Problem: The Philosophical Tradition We've now suggested that there is a crisis of community in contemporary society, *and* we've offered a focus on piety as an antidote for that crisis. What we have yet to do is to consider higher education; the reason, after all, that we're gathered here today. Is education part of the problem in teaching for piety (or community), or is it part of the solution? The answer to both, I would argue, is "yes."

In an interesting volume entitled *Orators and Philosophers; A History of Liberal Education*,[18] Bruce Kimball posits the existence of two traditions of liberal arts, the philosophical and the rhetorical. The former, which begins with Socrates, continues with the medieval scholastics, the Enlightenment *Philosophes*, and the modern university. Its goal is the unbounded search for knowledge and truth; it is characterized by an emphasis on intellect and rationality, critical scepticism, tolerance, individualism, and a strong commitment to the disciplines. The rhetorical tradition, in contrast, begins with Isocrates, and continues through Cicero and Quintilian, the Church Fathers, the Renaissance humanists, and the church-related liberal arts colleges. Its goal is to train good citizens to lead society; it is characterized by an emphasis on virtue, values and standards for character and conduct, tradition, communities of learning, an agreed-upon body of texts, and the central role of language.

Kimball is not suggesting that one of these traditions is uniformly good and one is evil, nor would I. His point is that there is a healthy tension between the two traditions, and I would add that embracing and acknowledging that tension helps keep each tradition from the evils of excess. But we're focusing this morning on the issue of community. Note that Kimball places the contemporary university in the philosophical tradition, and he suggests that that tradition has a clear

---

in the place of what has been destroyed," ibid.

[18](New York: Teachers College Press, 1986).

emphasis on individualism. How is it that the university model militates against community, and against piety?

I think it's fair to say that there is a tendency in the secular university to deny transcendence (recall Proctor's comment about religious studies cited above), but the university also works against piety by demanding objectivity. Nancey Murphy reminded us last night that during the Enlightenment, there was a "turn away from the authority of tradition and community. The self became the new focus and the new authority."[19] Partisanship was *verboten*. Absolute objectivity was necessary so that each autonomous self could develop for itself.

And the university militates against *community* by demanding ever more specialization. Specialization serves to destroy (or at least severely limit) dialogue, and it complicates efforts to forge a common agenda. I remember a Bethel graduate in chemistry who had gone off to earn his Ph.D. at a Big Ten university. When he returned to Bethel for a visit, I asked him if graduate school had held any big surprises for him. "There is one," he admitted. "I thought there was a reasonable chance that the chemists wouldn't spend much time with the physicists," he said, "but I was totally unprepared for the fact that the organic chemists won't even talk to the inorganic chemists!"

Second, the commitment to specialization drives the general concern for research over teaching. Later I will suggest that really good teachers have a deep concern for their students' lives outside the classroom. In the research cauldron that is the modern university, there is sometimes precious little concern for students *inside* the classroom, much less outside. Don't misunderstand me here. I know there are exceptions. I suspect all of us in this room can point to exceptions in our own graduate education experience. My friend Butch is an exception (which is one of the reasons I chose to begin these remarks with his story). But I also get the clear sense when I talk with Butch that he *is* an exception, that he is fundamentally lonely at Toronto, that his view of university education is distinctly counter-cultural in that environment.

Third, the commitment to specialization feeds arrogance. With enough specialized research, one can finally reach the point where one knows more than anyone else in the country about one infinitesimally small minutia of the human experience. And we are often very quick to

---

[19]Charles Scriven, "Schooling for the Tournament of Narratives: Postmodernism and the Idea of the Christian College," in *Theology Without Foundations: Religious Practice and the Future of Theological Truth*, edited by Stanley Hauerwas, Nancey Murphy, and Mark Nation (Nashville: Abingdon Press, 1994), 280.

generalize our expertise. If I clearly know more than you do about A, it's a fairly small leap (and perhaps a fundamental characteristic of the human condition) for me to assume that I probably know more than you do about B through Z as well.

Fourth, the commitment to specialization contributes to the cult of contemporaneity. In a specialist culture, the tendency is almost invariably to assume that the newest is the truest.

Fifth, the commitment to specialization may feed a tendency to view knowledge as a commodity, a collection of discrete packages of information. This leads to an arguably "counter-community" educational practice, distance learning. The vaunted Internet, that "Holy Grail" of contemporary educational technocrats, serves to divorce personality from the educational process (all interaction is mediated by the technology, there is no handwriting, no body language, no physical appearance). Moreover, according to Sherry Turkle's analysis in *Life on the Screen: Identity in the Age of the Internet*, it may lead to the development of "multiple personalities" that change with each "chat room" entered.[20] Try dealing with *that* kind of diversity in the search for the common story, commitments, and agenda that we determined to be essential for meaningful community!

But this is all someone else's problem, isn't it? All of us here represent church-related, Christian colleges and universities, institutions that fit squarely into Kimball's rhetorical tradition. We're not flirting brazenly with that philosophical tradition. Or are we? Is your college more or less discipline-focused than it was twenty-five

---

[20]Sherry Turkle, *Life on the Screen: Identity in the Age of the Internet* (New York: Simon & Schuster, 1995). The entire book deals with this issue; the following quote from an Internet user named Doug may serve as a representative sample: Doug talks about playing his characters in windows and says that using windows has made it possible for him to "turn pieces of my mind on and off. I split my mind. I'm getting better at it. I can see myself as being two or three or more. And I just turn on one part of my mind and then another when I go from window to window. I'm in some kind of argument in one window and trying to come on to a girl in a MUD in another, and another window might be running a spreadsheet program or some other technical thing for school . . . . And then I'll get a real-time message [that flashes on the screen as soon as it is sent from another system user], and I guess that's RL. It's just one more window." "RL is just one more window," he repeats, "and it's not usually my best one" 13. Turkle has also contributed a single-article adaptation from *Life on the Screen* entitled "Virtuality and Its Discontents: Searching for Community in Cyberspace," *The American Prospect*, no. 24 (Winter 1996): 50-57.

years ago? Is your curriculum more or less specialized? Has there been an increase or a decrease in common experiences for all students? Common texts? Does your institution have a common style manual, or do certain disciplines demand their own? Are you experimenting with distance learning?

And how about the objectivity question? I'd be interested to know how much surprise you experienced when I revealed Butch Goering's stated desire to "promote piety" among his students. Were you more surprised that a secular university professor was interested in promoting piety, or were you more shocked that *any* academic would be so unabashedly partisan, on any topic?

What I'm obviously intimating here is that we've all "bought into" that philosophical tradition to a greater or lesser degree. Why? I can think of a few obvious reasons. First, remember that the tradition is not evil. It has much to recommend it, though it appears to be counterproductive for community formation. Second, we've all been trained in that tradition, at least at the graduate level, and we've been good students. We've learned our lessons well. Third, I suspect that a growing number of our constituents expect, and even demand, that tradition. A Mennonite pastor once suggested to me that "Mennonites don't worship God anymore, they worship their children."[21] And if junior wants to go to Kansas State University, and if you really want him to go to Bethel College, you may well exert whatever pressure you can to make Bethel reflect K-State. Finally, along with its clear emphasis on community, it is also true that sixteenth-century Anabaptism required free conviction in the choice of religion. The roots of individualism have always been present in our peculiar religious heritage; never before, perhaps, have they been so assiduously watered and fertilized by the surrounding culture.

Education as Solution: The Rhetorical Tradition If the church-related liberal arts colleges are now taking too eagerly their cues from the universities, thereby slipping deeper into the philosophical tradition of liberal education, maybe we need to hark back to an earlier manifestation of the rhetorical tradition, the Renaissance humanists. The Renaissance humanists had their own version of the modern university with which to contend: medieval scholasticism. Scholasticism, you may recall, was the prevailing intellectual system in Western

---

[21]You see, that catechism of "No Fear" may also mean that children have no fear of their parents either. Perhaps that helps explain why parents are so quick to let their children make the college choice without parental counsel!

Europe from the eleventh through the fifteenth centuries. It was an elaborate attempt to reconcile faith and reason; it was heavily based on logic and dialectic; it gave us some of the finest minds in the history of civilization with men like Abelard, Anselm, Peter Lombard, and Butch's friend, Thomas Aquinas; and it provided the intellectual and philosophical foundation for the medieval Roman Catholic church. By 1500, however, scholasticism was in decline, in part because it had simply become too specialized, too esoteric, too abstruse, too "irrelevant." A marvellous example of this involves the wonderful, and almost-certainly apocryphal, story told by one Giraldus Cambrensis.[22]

It is the story of a young man who returned home after spending five years studying at the University of Paris, one of the last bastions of medieval scholasticism. The morning after his arrival, he and his father sat down at the breakfast table. On the table was a bowl containing six hard-boiled eggs. Much to the father's dismay, the son proceeded to demonstrate with remorseless logic that there were actually twelve eggs in the bowl instead of six. When the father had heard all he could tolerate, he proceeded to eat the six eggs he could see, leaving the other six for his son. (As absurd as this story sounds, I wonder how dissimilar would be the reaction of the father of a first-generation college student to that student's animated discourse on deconstructionist literary theory or postmodern epistemologies!?!) Robert Proctor has argued, perhaps unfairly, that for medieval scholastics the purpose of education was to make people *learned*, to ensure that in the exercise of their minds they could display their erudition, irrespective of the content of the exercise. If Proctor is correct (and I'm quite certain my friend Butch would question that assumption), the story told by Giraldus is a marvellously apt description of scholastic goals.

This is the educational vision challenged by the humanists, those sixteenth-century men (and even some women) committed to the *studia humanitatis*—the study of the humanities: grammar, literature, history, moral philosophy. Universally, and in some cases *profoundly* Christian, the humanists were interested in the recovery, the re-discovery of the original classical and Christian sources of Western civilization. *Ad fontes* ("to the sources") was their rallying cry. They would have been mortified at the thought of reading glosses of scholars on some original text (either Plato or the New Testament) rather than reading the original

---

[22]Will Durant, *The Age of Faith* (New York: Simon and Schuster, 1950), 982.

text itself. Their favourite tools were rhetoric and philology rather than logic and dialectic. They were fascinated with language, with its power and its beauty, in both its classical and vernacular forms. And they were especially concerned with behaviour, with ethics, with morality. They were much more interested in seeing how a man behaved than in hearing what he believed. They looked to models of behaviour in the past (e.g., Cicero, Socrates, or Jesus Christ) to provide guidance for how to behave in the present. Proctor argues that in contrast to the scholastics, the humanists believed that the fundamental purpose of education was to make people *good*.

Not surprisingly, their educational practice began with educating for piety. In 1530 Erasmus outlined the purposes of education as follows:

> The task of fashioning the young is made up of many parts, *the first and most important of which consists of implanting the seeds of* piety *in the tender heart*, the second in instilling a love for, and thorough knowledge of, the liberal arts; the third in giving instruction in the duties of life; the fourth in training in good manners right from the very earliest years.[23]

It's all here, isn't it? The initial emphasis on piety which seeks to instill respect for the past, devotion to God, and following after Christ; a broad-based education which encourages and supports dialogue across the disciplines; a concern for good manners and civility, which ensures that such dialogue can proceed appropriately.

If we're willing to embrace this model of education, how would we go about teaching it? How does one teach for piety? I invite you to consider 1) the professor as partisan, 2) the professor as model, and 3) the professor as pastor.

The professor as partisan.[24] There is a marvellous essay in

---

[23]Desiderius Erasmus, *On Good Manners for Boys,* vol. 25 of *Collected Works of Erasmus*, edited by J. K. Sowards (Toronto: University of Toronto Press, 1985), 273.

[24]I confess to some considerable discomfort with the word "partisan." It's nicely alliterative, and it *is* the term Scriven uses, so I have kept it. It does, however, imply a level of zealousness that is positively dangerous. The *Oxford English Dictionary* makes reference to "a blind, prejudiced, unreasoning, or fanatical adherent." *Merriam-Webster's Dictionary of Synonyms* suggests that "it often . . . connotes bigotry or prejudice." I would hope that being a "partisan for piety," at least in the sense of attempting "to be joined together with God through the imitation of Jesus Christ," would preclude one from exhibiting these more extreme manifestations of partisanship.

Theology Without Foundations: Religious Practice & the Future of Theological Truth, edited by Hauerwas, Nation, and our delightful keynote speaker for this gathering, Nancey Murphy. The essay is by Charles Scriven, and it is entitled, "Schooling for the Tournament of Narratives: Postmodernism and the Idea of the Christian College."[25] I frankly suspect Erasmus and the Renaissance humanists would find the discussion of postmodernism a bit too scholastic-sounding for their liking, but I'm confident they would enthusiastically affirm the *behaviours* that Scriven prescribes.

Scriven argues that Christian colleges must educate in a way that is decidedly partisan, in a way that "honors and reflects the church's narrative," in a way that "not only display[s] . . . the church's true identity," but in a way that represents "a deliberate strategy for building and bracing the circle of disciples."[26] Such an approach would be markedly counter-cultural in the university-based, Enlightenment-driven, philosophical tradition. Scriven quotes a professor at a Southern Baptist college who revealed his Enlightenment presuppositions when he declared, "It's not my job as a professor to tell [students] what to think, it's my job to *make* them think."[27] Scriven suggests that such an argument is fundamentally vacuous. In a "tournament of narratives," he says, "the point . . . is not *whether* to be partisan but *how*."[28]

Scriven is not through with us yet. "Suspicion of commitment in the classroom," he writes, "does not, of course, produce students with no biases at all; it rather favors their 'assimilation . . . to the prevailing cultural ethos.'"[29] Anne Matthews of New York University has recently written a powerful description of higher education entitled *Bright College Years*. In discussing "the campus after dark," she describes a world that most professors do not know exists—perhaps can scarcely even imagine existing, because it is so at variance with what they are

---

[25]Stanley Hauerwas, Nancey Murphy, Mark Nation, eds., *Theology Without Foundations: Religious Practice & the Future of Theological Truth* (Nashville, TN: Abingdon Press, 1994), 273-288.

[26]Ibid., 274.

[27]Ibid., 275.

[28]Ibid., 277.

[29]Ibid., 280.

trying to teach in the classroom.[30] If these behaviours result from the fact that the real catechism for our students is popular culture, and if Scriven is right that our feigned objectivity is actually working to reinforce, rather than counteract, those behaviours, we had best resolve to become much more explicit and partisan in expressing in the classroom our commitment to piety.[31]

---

[30]*Bright College Years: Inside the American Campus Today* (New York: Simon & Schuster, 1997), see especially, 84-108. While I would freely (and thankfully) admit that on Mennonite campuses "the campus after dark" is a problem of lesser magnitude than the national norm, I would also contend that the difference is one of degree not of substance. (Note: On p. 84, Matthews comments that "In a generation light on heroes and heroines, the college-age turn to each other, and sometimes turn on each other." I would argue that this generation is "light on heroes and heroines," in no small part, because of the cult of contemporaneity discussed earlier.)

[31]I would like to offer a homely example of this partisanship at work. I ask you to consider the Bethel College Concert Choir. The Choir sings only sacred repertoire. Its director, Dr. Marles Preheim, has occasionally expressed some frustration over that fact. "There is," he says, "lots of great secular music out there, and I sometimes feel like I'm shortchanging our music majors by sending them out into the field with so little exposure to it." But we are, after all, a Christian college, and 95 percent of our performance venues are sacred settings, so Marles sticks with the sacred repertoire. That's partisanship.

Does it have an impact? I think it does. One of the joys of my current job portfolio is planning spring break choir tours to constituent churches and accompanying the choir on those tours. In preparation, I always tell the choir that there is no group I would rather take on the road as a representative of Bethel College than the Concert Choir. I say it partly to boost morale, to generate *esprit de corps* for the "grueling task" ahead. But I mostly say it because it is true. And it is true for two reasons. First, our constituent churches love nothing more than outstanding choral music, and over the years we've been able to consistently provide same. Second, at least in my experience, the choir members have behaved uncommonly well on those tours—much better, I think, than a random group of 40-50 students; better even, I think, than any other group of students (e.g., athletic team, forensics team, etc.). I am repeatedly thanked by hotel clerks, restaurant cashiers, for accompanying such an unusually responsible and well-behaved group. Now, don't get me wrong. I'm not totally naive. I am quite sure that things happen of which I am not aware and would not approve. I'm sure much of the music they are listening to on their Walkmans while they ride the bus—as well as most of the movies they watch on that bus—do much more to reinforce the catechism of popular culture than they do for teaching piety. But I also know that when you have to leave a hotel in downtown San Francisco at 7:00 a.m. after a night in which the

The professor as model. We need to remember again the old aphorism that "values are caught, not taught." Thus *who* is teaching a given course, and *how* that course is taught may well be more important than the specific subject matter of the course. If I may again use Butch as an example: For years Butch taught a very popular course at the University of Toronto called "The History of War." He once commented to me that there were always some Mennonites in the course, and they were almost invariably the ones who first figured out what was really going on. Four or five weeks into the semester, they would stop him in the hall after class and say, "Dr. Goering, this course is really about the "history of peace," isn't it?" I am not one to consider content or curriculum as fundamentally irrelevant; I have just argued that we have an obligation to teach students *what* to think as well as how to think. My point here is simply that a course in "Analytical Chemistry" taught by the "right" faculty member may have more potential for teaching for piety (or community) than a course in "Principles of Piety" or "Community-Building 101" taught by the wrong faculty member. (In fact, if you want to have the most impact on the most students, the last thing you may want to do is offer a course in "Principles of Piety." In the words of Butch Goering, "If I had called the course 'The History of Peace,' I would likely have spent the whole semester preaching to the converted." There is something to be said for indirect approaches to issues that really matter, which may be yet

---

students were totally on their own, and when every student is down in the lobby, bright-eyed and bushy-tailed, waiting for the bus with all luggage in hand at 6:30 a.m., this is a very special group of students.

Why? Here's my theory. I think it's related to the fact that they sing only sacred repertoire. Last month I had the privilege of singing with the choir under the direction of Vance George (Goshen alumnus who conducts the San Francisco Symphony Chorus) for our Mother's Day concert. We were singing Poulenc's "Gloria," and Vance, in an effort to get the sound he wanted, was *constantly* reminding us to think about the words we were singing. It's not a concept unique to Vance George. Every conductor does it. Marles Preheim does it. That means, of course, that these concert choir members are reminded virtually every day at rehearsal to "think" and then sing pious thoughts. Most of you have been in choirs. You know that the injunction to "think about what you're singing" frequently falls on deaf ears. But my hypothesis is that it makes a difference. Put another way, I am willing to suggest that if you took that same group of students on that same tour singing only Broadway show tunes (or worse, some of the stuff they were likely listening to on their Walkmans), we would have had significant behavior problems to deal with on the tour. If my hypothesis is true, we will have learned something about teaching for piety.

another argument for approaching the issue of community indirectly, through piety.) My colleagues in educational psychology, incidentally, assure me that the social scientific data confirms the truth of this aphorism, in that professors who model or "embody" the principles they profess are much more successful teachers than those who do not.

And this modelling behaviour must continue outside the classroom as well as inside. We spoke earlier of the need for meaningful conversation, civility, and humility. If values are caught, not taught, faculty and staff at our colleges need to be modelling this behaviour *consistently*! I don't know all that much about "influence," but my strong hunch is that it most often happens unawares. You're probably having the least influence on others when you're convinced you're having the most, and vice-versa.

The professor as pastor. I will go even further. If we are to educate effectively for piety (perhaps if we are to educate effectively, period), I believe that, in addition to their intellectual role, faculty and staff at our colleges need to assume a pastoral role. What does that mean? To me it suggests that 1) faculty should have an explicit concern for, and a positive impact on, faith development; and 2) faculty should be concerned about, even involved in, their students' lives outside of classroom in the same way that a pastor is concerned about the lives of her "flock" outside the church. I am well aware that this is no easy task. More than one academic, upon hearing this argument, has suggested that the "academic" personality is, almost by definition, strikingly "unpastoral." I wouldn't argue that these kinds of folks are easy to find; I would contend, however, that these are precisely the kind of faculty our constituents expect to find when they send their children to their church colleges.[32]

Is there any "down side" here? Of course, there is. I suspect some faculty at our colleges would suggest that I have just dreamed the impossible dream and defined the impossible job. I take the critique seriously, but I would add that, in general, the professors who come the closest to accomplishing the role I just described appear to me to be the most energized and fulfilled persons on our faculty.

A second critique reveals what has always been the Achilles' heel of the rhetorical tradition: censorship and indoctrination. Charles Scriven

---

[32]One final aside, since we're talking about professors as pastors, here's a comment for pastors. Worship is by definition an exercise in teaching for piety defined as devotion for God. It is *not* by definition an exercise in teaching for piety defined as respect for the past. I am passionately convinced that the most effective and lasting worship does both!

acknowledges the tendency, but he rightly argues that being partisan need not "slump into narrow indoctrination."[33] And we know that it need not because the long history of the rhetorical tradition is full of examples of precisely the opposite.

Scriven introduces us to Origen, the third-century Greek Church Father.[34] Didymus the Blind called Origen "the greatest teacher in the Church after the apostles."[35] So how did he teach? Origen began by befriending his students. He "sought to change the lives of his students by establishing a personal and intimate relationship with them."[36] What did he teach? Everything. "No enquiry was closed to them, no knowledge was withheld from them (though they were *advised*—not *prohibited* from, but advised—not to waste time on any authors who denied the existence of any god). They had the chance to study every branch of learning, Greek or foreign, spiritual or sociological, human or divine."[37] At the same time, however, Origen was "unmistakably partisan."[38] Though he exposed his students to philosophy and poetry, geometry and astronomy, his school was a "training ground for Christianity,"[39] a school "for training in virtue," "whose goal was to form the lives of [its] students in light of the ideal set forth in the Scriptures and imaged in Christ."[40] "Supremely," says James McClendon, "he taught them that piety and scholarship were partners, not rivals."[41] Last, but certainly not least, he modeled what he taught. His students noted that he "stimulated us by the deeds he did more than

---

[33]Scriven, 284.

[34]Origen, incidentally, was one of Erasmus' two favorite Church Fathers (the other being Jerome). At the time of his death in 1536, Erasmus was working on a new edition of the writings of Origen.

[35]G. L. Prestige, *Fathers and Heretics: Six Studies in Dogmatic Faith with Prologue and Epilogue* (London: SPCK, 1963), 52.

[36]Robert L. Wilken, "Alexandria: A School for Training in Virtue," in *Schools of Thought in the Christian Tradition*, edited by Patrick Henry (Philadelphia: Fortress Press, 1984), 21.

[37]Prestige, 51.

[38]Scriven, 285.

[39]James Wm. McClendon, Jr., *Systematic Theology: Ethics* (Nashville: Abingdon Press, 1986), 43.

[40]Wilken, 19.

[41]McClendon, 43.

by the doctrines he taught."[42]

There have been countless others. Each of us could name examples from our own institutions who have done a spectacular job of teaching/modelling/pastoring for piety. They were invariably overworked and underpaid, but they were never unappreciated. I will close with part of a letter to one such teacher. In the interests of objectivity, I have not chosen a letter to a faculty member from one of the schools represented here today. In the interests of piety (respect for the past), I have chosen a letter written over 480 years ago. It came from the pen of one Heinrich Loriti Glareanus, a man who likely had at least some influence on everyone in this room, since he was Conrad Grebel's first—and, at least in one sense, favourite—college professor. On 5 September 1516, Glarean wrote his own teacher, Desiderius Erasmus.

> A great thing indeed it was to have learnt morals from Socrates and set one's life in order under his instructions; yet I have had far more from you—besides an infinity of other things, one above all, that you taught me to seek the philosophy of Christ, and not to seek that only but to imitate Him, to worship Him, to love Him. Could anything nobler or more profitable fall to the lot of an ordinary man like me? . . . It was not eloquence or learning on which you taught me to rely, it was on truly Christian love; and accordingly I owe you a debt of gratitude the most abundant, undying, superlative and all the other long words our common stylists are so fond of, and which (more to the point) I pray Christ may repay to you in view of all that you have done for me.[43]

I leave you this morning with Paul Oskar Kristeller's challenge: Are we, as educators at Mennonite colleges, proving to the future that we have lived up to the standards of the past?

----

[42]Ibid., 43.

[43]Glarean to Erasmus, 5 September 1516, in *The Correspondence of Erasmus*, vol. 4 (Toronto: University of Toronto Press, 1977), 69-70.

7 Mennonite Education Administration: An Inside View

Joseph L. Lapp[1]

Introduction I commented to my wife Hannah several weeks ago about needing to figure out what to say in this address about administration and she replied: "You ought to know because this is your life." Sometime later I was at a meeting where one of our associate trustees asked me how it is going. I replied, "I reckon it is okay." And she went on to say, "You seem to get what you want in a nice way." I haven't figured out if this was a compliment or criticism. Knowing the person, I have taken it as a compliment.

In my student years I did not prepare for educational administration, nor did I study the theories of education. But now after ten years of experience, I would consider myself a modest practitioner of educational administration. My self-evaluation or perception of these ten years is fairly positive. Neither have I been specifically educated as a theologian, at least not at the graduate level, yet I have developed a modicum of understanding of the church and theology as a lay person.

Having stated what I am not, you might understand if I misstate any theology, education, or administration theory. The challenge that administrators of Mennonite colleges face is to communicate how these elements are held together.

The question before us is: "What makes a college, university or seminary Mennonite?" I don't intend to answer this question but I am hoping that after hearing the various presentations we may develop some consensus regarding key characteristics.

---

[1]President, Eastern Mennonite University, Harrisonburg, Virginia.

My intention is to have you think with me in several areas. First, I would like to use my experience and the history of Eastern Mennonite University (EMU) as a frame of reference. Secondly, I will make a few comments about certain qualities that generally inform administrators of Mennonite institutions. Thirdly, I will consider organizational structures in Mennonite institutions and, fourthly, I will state particular challenges faced by administrators at Mennonite institutions.

A Brief Historical Perspective of EMU and My Personal Experience Permit me to provide a few facts regarding my personal experience that may have some connection to my work as an administrator at EMU. *First,* all of my education from elementary through college was in Mennonite schools. *Second,* I was born and raised in the family of a Mennonite Church leader. From childhood my life was Mennonite Church, its people, and its organizations. *Third,* after college, as a young adult, I felt the need to do something different from other family members and so I went to law school. Following law school I practiced law for 15 years in eastern Pennsylvania--in perhaps the original Mennonite colony in North America. *Fourth,* I was admitted to the Bar for the practice of law at the age of 29 and the following year, in 1973, I was elected a trustee of EMU. *Fifth,* after two years I was elected chair of the academics committee of the trustees and vice chair of the board and thus became a member of the executive committee. *Sixth,* after seven years on the board I was elected chair and served in that capacity until 1986 when I became president-elect. In 1987 I assumed the office of president of EMU. *Seventh,* coming from a large family of siblings, many of whom entered Mennonite educational institutions ahead of me, I learned much by listening to the conversations about institutional life—specifically about the issues between faculty and administrators. I developed perceptions about people and events, obviously cloaked in the perspective of the persons communicating the comments. *Eighth,* as a trustee I continued to hear from many of my friends in my home area concerning how things ought to be in a Mennonite school. Before and since becoming president, I have been actively involved as a lay person in traditional Mennonite communities. *Ninth,* my memory of the first several years on the Eastern Mennonite trustee board is rather poor. I do remember, however, that in those first several years I was slightly intimidated. I was the youngest trustee until Elvin Kraybill was elected several years later. The trustees were mostly white, male church-types—pastors, or church organization staff—with a few business persons and a few medical doctors who had been former missionaries.

From its beginning and into the 1970s, Eastern Mennonite was independent of the Mennonite Board of Education (MBE). Al Meyer, then executive secretary of MBE, attended the trustee meetings very regularly. Soon after I became vice chair of the board, Al Meyer began to target me and co-opted me as part of his strategy to bring Eastern Mennonite under the MBE umbrella. When Richard Detweiler became president in 1980, he may have been targeted as part of the Meyer strategy as well.

In 1978-1979 after much discussion among trustees and within the Constituent Conference Committee, Eastern Mennonite entered into a three-year covenant relationship with MBE which Al Meyer spelled out in a detailed agreement. This began a kind of engagement period between Eastern Mennonite and MBE.

This covenant relationship was extended several years and in 1984 Eastern Mennonite formally joined MBE, revising our corporate charter and bylaws, restructuring the board of trustees, agreeing to the division of duties and responsibilities for MBE and Eastern Mennonite and we began paying our dues.

A Few Comments about Eastern Mennonite's History
Eastern Mennonite began in 1917 as a Bible academy. Later it became a junior college, and then a senior college in 1948. It achieved regional accreditation in 1959. The seminary began in 1948, and several additional graduate programs were added in 1990s. The university name was adopted in the 1990s.

During the first approximately 65 years of our history, Virginia Mennonite Conference owned and governed Eastern Mennonite School/Eastern Mennonite College & Seminary. In the first half of our history, Eastern Mennonite was a primary agenda item of the annual assembly of Virginia Mennonite Conference. The president was frequently required to explain or interpret occurrences at Eastern Mennonite.

This was direct grassroots governance of higher education. In these first fifty years the trustees were basically a self-perpetuating board electing members from nominations received from Virginia Conference.

As a young distant observer, I remember hearing of something called RWC and frequently not in very complimentary terms. The RWC was the Religious Welfare Committee, a board committee appointed by the Virginia Mennonite Conference to interview and approve all prospective faculty. This was one of the ways in which the local conference maintained ownership and governance of the school.

Gradually Virginia Conference was able to have other conferences on the east coast nominate persons for service on the board of trustees. It was in the 1960s that several representatives were appointed from other eastern conferences.

During the 1950s to the 1970s while Eastern Mennonite was maturing as a school, the Virginia Conference was also changing. The conference began to give more attention to matters other than Eastern Mennonite. It was during this time that Virginia Conference began developing its own independent mission program. The conference explored sending missionaries to Jamaica and also to Italy. I have wondered whether there was a direct connection between the development of new vision within the conference and the reduced focus on Eastern Mennonite.

Another observation may be that Eastern Mennonite also broadened its vision. Enrollment grew, new programs were introduced and regional accreditation was achieved in 1959. New presidential leadership in 1965 with Myron Augsburger also brought a more expansive vision.

In the early 80s, when I returned to my law office following trustee meetings, my partner Richard Rosenberger who chaired the board of trustees at Bluffton College, would often ask me how things were in Harrisonburg. My response was frequently, "okay—except a few million dollars would certainly improve things." When I was appointed president in 1986, there seemed to be three significant weaknesses at Eastern Mennonite that I believed would require special effort.

First, in 1986-1987 Eastern Mennonite experienced the lowest enrollment since the late 60s or early 70s. Increased enrollment, in my opinion, was crucial for the future health of the school.

Second, financial support was an ongoing struggle. The endowment was low and the expected annual fund was large. Special attention would need to be given to fundraising.

Third, even though the school was noted for high faculty morale, in a mid 1980s study by the Council of Independent Colleges, there seemed to be an internal lack of confidence and more than a reasonable ability to think everyone else was doing much better. This strong feeling of inferiority seemed inappropriate in my opinion.

Though these weaknesses seemed very significant, I was convinced there were good programs and good people in place to move the school forward.

How Mennonite Institutions Inform the Way we Function as Administrators
Here I will probably get in over my head. There are probably historians, sociologists, and theologians who know more about these areas than I will cover in broad strokes. I will make a few comments about Mennonite institutions historically, about our social context, and then about our theology. It seems to me that our tradition, derived from our history, social context and theology, informs the way

we function as administrators—especially if we have Anabaptist roots, which many of us do. These areas—history, social context and theology—in my opinion frequently form a framework for administrators of a Mennonite institution. This framework exists almost intuitively because of how we are so inextricably rooted in our history, social context and theology. I will let you make the direct connections to institutional function.

First, historical factors. Anabaptists have a sense of suffering that is passed down through the generations. Though in the 20th century we have not concentrated as much on our martyr history, the reformation history has provided moving illustrations as we continue to research and tell our story. Our 20th century, however, has not provided much suffering.

Another part of our history could be identified as "people on the move." Prior to coming to North America many Anabaptists moved for the purpose of finding relative freedom to live their faith. In North America in our first several centuries there has been movement of Anabaptists across the continent and even today amongst our Amish brothers and sisters there continues to be community relocation occurring. In this century some of this movement happened as we discovered opportunities as a result of conscription for alternate service as Conscientious Objectors (COs).

Our agrarian history, now practically forgotten in many eastern communities, was very formative in the creation of who we are. Many of us have a sense of belonging to the land. We think about land ownership quantitatively. Many of us are not comfortable long-term apartment dwellers.

Anabaptists are relative late-comers to higher education. It is my sense that our Anabaptist higher education institutions still have a higher than average percentage of first generation college/university students.

Periodically throughout our history there has been an intentional rekindling of our faith history within us as a people. My generation in this century experienced Bender's restatement of the Anabaptist Vision. This periodic recollection of where we came from, who we are and then creating a new vision, has revitalized our people throughout the centuries. For church leadership we have long felt that studies in Anabaptist history were important ingredients of an educational curriculum.

Second, social context. Our schools of higher education have developed in geographic regions where there was an Anabaptist community. Until the last several decades of this century, most of these communities could be identified with the characteristics of most ethnic groups. Eastern Mennonite developed in the midst of a period of Anabaptist separatism—at least on the east coast.

With this separatist identity in the early 20th century, Anabaptists organized elementary and secondary educational institutions and other social services as well. Now at the end of the century, without the traditional community characteristics and without this separatist value, our social context creates ambiguity as to who we are as we have assimilated into the larger North American culture.

Third, theology. The origins of our Mennonite schools are integrally tied into our interests of preserving and passing on our faith and practice. Our theological orientation has consistently been rooted in the Christian Bible. Our emphasis is on preserving Jesus' teaching concerning nonresistant peace, mutual care for others within the community, concern for the physical and spiritual condition of the world around us, and a sense of witness by "being" and "doing."

Sometimes our theological purposes have been to distinguish Anabaptists from other Christians, and at other times to distinguish more specifically among Anabaptist groups. One of our faculty has argued that our only unique value is a nonviolent approach to all we do.

Theologically most of us in this century went about our educational task as schools attempting to be unique while doing educationally what others were doing. By requiring faculty, chief administrators and board members to be Mennonite Church members, Mennonite institutions tried to maintain theological integrity.

During this first 100 years of Anabaptist higher education, each of our institutions has developed a corporate culture from the weaving together of history, social context and theology, perpetuating the initiatives of institutional founders and subsequent interpreters of these threads. Institutional corporate culture that develops from this weaving together of history, social context and theology seems to sustain an institution for a long time. The terms we use to describe our respective missions, I believe, come from who we have been and want to be—Anabaptist, communities, service oriented, peacemakers, etc.

It seems to me that at the end of the 20th century the way in which these threads have been woven together for most of the century, is now being rewoven or realigned. As to history, we are searching for a new Anabaptist vision and identity.

The social context and orientation for Anabaptist people is changing/has changed drastically. We are less agrarian, less land oriented, there are fewer characteristics of a cohesive community, and there is more assimilation into the larger culture.

Theologically we are trying to determine whether we are Christian, evangelical Christian, evangelical Anabaptist, Anabaptist, or Mennonites or something else. The question is: Are we unique—should we be unique as Anabaptists?

Frequently I hear people say, "Our time—the end of the 20th century—is more _____ than at any other time in history." Perhaps we can thus say, "our time" as Anabaptist higher education educators is one requiring us to be informed with several important convictions like: a new sense of our history as a people of faith, a new understanding of how we can and ought to be a religious community, and a new identification of who we are as a people of faith.

It seems to me that we have done very well in creating a confession of faith adopted by the Mennonite Church and the General Conference Mennonite Church. This goes a long way in providing a theological understanding of who we are. We need to continue to connect with our history and develop new characteristics for the community we want to be.

These broad strokes, I am sure, leave much to be desired. What does this have to do with function? The functional issue for administrators can be stated in several ways: Who/what is a Mennonite? Is it important to be a "card-carrying" Mennonite?

Most of us as administrators attempt to project internally—on campus—and externally—among our constituent groups—our institution-al identity as Christians in the Anabaptist-Mennonite tradition. As we work at issues of identity we are all well aware of the diversity of religious traditions in our respective academic communities. That also means diversity within the Anabaptist-Mennonite tradition. On occasion when someone indicates a weakness in our Anabaptist identity, we identify and defend the existence of our Anabaptist uniqueness. On those occasions when someone challenges our lack of diversity, we roll out statistics that point to our pluralism. Some applicants for positions seem to rather easily state their agreement with Mennonite faith and practice. I recognize that "faith and practice" in the abstract or on paper is different from faith and practice that develops from decades of living and working together. Some Mennos try to shake off the Menno traditions of faith and practice. Some OTMs provide insightful ways of renewing traditional faith and practice.

At Eastern Mennonite we try to weave together Anabaptist history, Anabaptist social context, and Anabaptist theology in our general education curriculum and in numerous elective courses. Through campus ministry program, extra curricular activities, and the modelling and mentoring of a predominately Anabaptist-Mennonite faculty and staff, we hope the abstract becomes a reality.

Even with such intentionality other competing forces exist. There remains a kind of intuitive nature of educators that tends to pull us toward academic excellence creating pressure to conform to mainstream educational norms. This seemingly intuitive force creates a constant tension with the goal of being uniquely Christian in the Anabaptist tradition. At EMU Dean Hawk speaks of "faithful practice that informs learning and learning that transforms faith." Those of us on the inside of Anabaptist higher education think that our "faithful practice informs learning and learning transforms faith" in the intentional ways I identified at EMU and the numerous "soft"-indirect ways as Christian discipleship, are modeled and mentored in the academic community.

Only last week a pastor of some experience and an alumnus of EMU visited with me just to make sure we have not lost our intentionality about being Christian. A major area that informs administrators is what we perceive to be the "state of the church." We must work with the students the church sends us.

In summary on this point: as one of the Mennonite Church higher education institutions, I think "being" a Mennonite-Anabaptist institution is frequently brought into focus for community awareness, occasionally more than some faculty and staff think necessary. The major benefit, however, in maintaining this heavy emphasis on being Mennonite, is that we acknowledge the "oughtness" and need to maintain a unique identity for the University. I, for one, have frequently said, "If we do not have a unique identity as an institution, there is little reason for us to exist. There are many other excellent universities—we don't need to make the significant investment we are making if we do not have unique qualities."

Should Our Organizational Structures Be Designed in Particular Ways to Reflect Our Understanding of Being Mennonite Institutions   There is probably no correct answer to this question. Mennonite institutions have for a long time been organized in many different ways. There is little, if anything, that would indicate that there is a correct structure to reflect our understanding of being Mennonite Schools.

I am choosing to approach the issue of organizational structure from my experience with EMU. This experience frequently places me "on the fence." As stated earlier, a major issue across North America among Anabaptists-Mennonites is: By what criteria should an organization be classified as "Mennonite" or "Anabaptist"? There are many organizational structures used across North America: Mennonite self-sustaining boards; Mennonite patron appointed boards; Mennonite conference-appointed boards; Mennonite named organizations but with few Mennonite staff, residences, clients, etc.

In the late 1970s a new retirement community was being developed in Montgomery County, Pennsylvania. As an attorney and as a member of the Franconia Mennonite Conference, I cautioned that direct lines of accountability to the local Mennonite conference might create the attachment of legal liability. This occurred soon after a major liability claim had been levied against the United Methodists as a result of a retirement community using the denominational name "Methodist" and allegedly failed to meet agreements with its clients.

As I recall, the Dock Woods Community was created with a relationship to the Franconia Mennonite Conference but without conference control or governance. The Dock Woods Community has developed very successfully and I understand from an attorney friend on the board that it is generally considered a "Mennonite institution" though its percentage of Mennonite residents probably does not exceed 25 percent. Most of the administration and board would be members of local Mennonite congregations which are part of Franconia Mennonite Conference.

From my experience and observations during the past number of years, the parts of the organizational structure most important in making any institution Mennonite are: 1) the mission and vision that catches the core of Mennonite faith and practice more for philosophical accountability than for ownership and governance; 2) trustees or boards of directors who are Mennonite in faith and practice; 3) administrators who are Mennonite in faith and practice; 4) persons in other key mission defining positions who are Mennonite in faith and practice; and 5) a program that incorporates intentionally the values and essentials of Mennonite faith and practice. All the above persons must be able to connect with the specific mission of the school.

So for us as Mennonite educators, I believe the organizational criteria for our colleges, universities, seminaries could be stated similarly. First, a mission that provides an education consistent with Mennonite faith and practice. And, I would be bold enough to suggest, minimizing "ownership and governance" language. Secondly, the organizational requirements for carrying out such a mission seem to be a board, administrators and a faculty majority that clearly understands and accepts the educational mission and Christian faith and practice as expressed in the Anabaptist-Mennonite tradition.

Allow me to refer back to the history of EMU. The structure of Eastern Mennonite from 1917 to the 1960s identified the school with a local group of churches that, over time, developed—in my opinion—an unhealthy relationship. The local governance tended to maintain a narrow focus while the developing/maturing school, as naturally occurs in most developing organizations, was broadening/expanding in the world of knowledge and program development. The school needed more than regionally focused Virginia board members. Connections with the broader church and region later created incentives for the ultimate merger with MBE.

Gerald Gerbrandt made a reference to the Canadian schools being closely connected to congregations and conferences. Yet I would ask whether a congregation or conference can develop an adequate vision for schools as we think they should be? The focus for such independent schools seems inevitably to be limited to the immediate, local community frames of reference.

For several decades after broadening its governance from Virginia Conference to Mennonite conferences over the east coast, the trustees numbered 32 persons representing all the eastern conferences with a variety of persons, including educators, clergy/pastors, alumni and business persons. As part of the 32 trustees for more than 10 years, I found the large group inefficient, costly and cumbersome. However, the large number was helpful in representing the school across the region. This representative role to external constituents was as important as the representative role of the regions to the institution.

Our current board, as part of MBE, has a membership of 13 persons, is less costly and more efficient for processing business. It is difficult to maintain a board profile that adequately represents a large geographical region, provides adequately for church representation, as well as representation of professional educators, alumni, business and other professional interests. The smaller board clearly makes it more difficult to achieve the external representative function and the regional representation to the University which the larger board did by numbers.

Periodically, I feel EMU should have a larger number of trustees in order to: properly represent the broadened program and areas, i.e., undergrad, grad, seminary; have the appropriate voices in processing specialized agenda; adequately represent the university externally over the large geographic region; have a board that could financially provide more support for the university.

It seems to me, the issues of organizational structure for Mennonite institutions are not much different than for any organization in North America. The questions is: Who will the "constituently important" trust to hold an organization accountable to an approved mission? Church appointed people? Self appointed people? School appointed? Business persons? Does accountability for mission require a tightly integrated hierarchical pyramid?

Unique Challenges Facing Administrators of Mennonite Educational Institutions I will identify several areas where I think administrators of Mennonite educational institutions have unique challenges. Some of these may be common to all educators; however, they seem to be unique challenges that I have identified from my own experience as president.

Within the Mennonite denomination there seems to be a system of communication that functions very well to keep administrators on their toes. An event can occur at EMU and if it has negative connotations it will be heard throughout the constituency by one person saying to another, "Did you hear what happened at EMU?" Many schools with fewer denominational connections appear to have less concern with their dirty linen getting broadcast throughout their various constituencies. At EMU with the large majority of faculty and staff being Mennonite and almost 65 percent of our students being Mennonite, the communication channels are such that the church hears very quickly about anything, especially things with negative overtones.

A unique question for a denominational school is: What level of open communication should there be with the church. Should we hang out our dirty linen? In a sense every church member claims a voice in ownership and governance of MBE schools. The practical side of this is that each of the MBE schools exists as one entity held accountable by 1,100 congregations. When we, as individual schools in turn, look at who is holding us accountable we see 1,100 different congregations with great diversity in faithful practice.

In our attempt to be a university where "faithful practice informs learning and learning transforms faith" there ought to be lively, dynamic discussion of a wide range of subjects. In such a setting, a denominational university may be seen as pushing the edges too far. Can a denomination provide the freedom to be a Christian university—the freedom to engage in critical reflection without being subjected to an inquisition? Or, as asked this morning what is the defining tradition? Who defines the tradition? How many traditions can any one school allow to co-exist.

MBE April 4-5, 1997 minutes #15: "After discussion the MBE reiterated its position that respectful dialogue from various perspectives should be encouraged on campus within the parameters of Mennonite General Assembly statements. The MBE urges schools to maintain grounding in the life of the church even when this is difficult."

Administrators of denominationally owned and governed institutions such as we represent, are constantly trying to determine whether there is any freedom within denominational religious statements to explore agenda that seems to contravene denominational positions. Part of the issue is: Can a denomination allow for some of its brightest and best to think "new thoughts" without being subjected to charges of heresy?

As a Mennonite university, we frequently have been challenged for failing to use the discipline of Matthew 18. On several occasions we have been criticized for reporting incidents to the legal authorities for processing. In the context of a growing Anabaptist family, with some children having been nurtured in the faith in their childhood and some being struck by bolts of lightening and some intellectually choosing the Anabaptist way, administrators face the challenge of creating a harmonious family where the children have many diverse gifts.

A current challenge to the Mennonite Church and General Conference Mennonite Church administrators is what, if any, cooperative organization there should be for Mennonite education in the new integrated church. In my opinion a church is organizationally very different from a business corporation. Yet a program organization within the church structure may function similarly to a business corporation model. The question is: How do they relate? As a churchly organization mixing with a business corporate model?

Conclusion I am sure there is much more that could be said from an administrator's point of view. Many of you are or have been in administration and may have different experiences. I have glossed over many areas you may wish to pursue in more detail. Perhaps that can occur in our discussion.

----

8 Mennonite Education Administration: An Outside View

Ted Koontz[1]

Introduction The discussion of administration in church schools raises for me the deepest questions about Mennonite theology and ethics: Are they applicable, or are they simply pie in the sky? I hear loudly the voices of those who find an unbridgeable gulf between our "ideal" ethics and "real" life, especially in our institutions.

Implicit in what I write is a view that sees much wrong with our schools. This may have much to do with my academic training as a "realist" political scientist and my personality. Although I would like to be a "priest," my friends tell me I am mostly a "prophet," which I take to be a nice word for grouch! It also has to do with comparing our schools to a vision, not to other schools. When I do put on my comparative hat, I find much reason for gratitude in our schools, as well as many of our other institutions.[2]

I want to do several things in this essay. *First,* to share why I am convinced that thinking about administration Mennonite-Christianly is important for the integrity of the theological tradition in which we stand.

Second, to speak to how Mennoniteness does or does not, should or should not, shape the way we operate our institutions—the kind of institutions we *are*, not the content of what we teach, not our stated mission as much as the nature of our life together.

Third, to speak to the question of what I, as professor, want from

---

[1]Professor of Ethics and Peace Studies, Associated Mennonite Biblical Seminary.

[2]See Thomas Jeavons, *When the Bottom Line is Faithfulness: Management of Christian Service Organizations* (Bloomington, IN: Indiana University Press, 1994), for a comparison of MCC (though unnamed) with other Christian service organizations.

administrators, and what I want to give to them.

Fourth, to state why I think we have Mennonite schools.

The Centrality of Our Agenda Many of the questions from the planning document for the conference focus on connecting our faith to institutional life. The questions imply that there should be a connection, and that it should make a difference in the kind of schools we are.

But why does it matter to make this connection? Why not be just like any other good educational institution? And what are the particular challenges of connecting institutional life, the work of administrators in church related institutions, here schools, to our particular, peculiar theological-ethical heritage?

Let me begin by stating a conviction and a confession. I believe that the connection between our institutional reality and our theology constitutes a crucial test for the theological-ethical vision of those of us standing in the Anabaptist tradition. Can we find ways of thinking about, and operating, our church institutions that are congruent with our Anabaptist faith heritage? At stake for me is whether I can with integrity continue offering an Anabaptist alternative to other Christian traditions and their ways of doing social ethics, or whether I need to admit that we have been barking up the wrong theological tree for nearly five centuries and say, "You Lutherans, or Calvinists, or Catholics (but especially you Lutherans) were right all along." More on this later.

The confession is this. As pretentious or ridiculous or shallow as it may sound, I would like to be a saint, by which I mean, most simply, a single-minded and whole-hearted Christian. What, you may ask, does this confession have to do with my topic? Just as I would like to be a saint, so I would like our church institutions to be saintly. I know how strange, perhaps laughable, or perhaps deeply painful, this may sound to some of us with our sometimes difficult experiences with our institutions. Nevertheless, I believe our institutions should be saintly. They should be windows through which others see the joyful, new-making power of Christ's gospel exemplified in their very "being"—not only in their mission or their words, but in the shape and quality of their shared corporate life. Creating saintly institutions is a substantial challenge for our school administrators, one that I doubt has appeared on any presidential job description!

Just as Anabaptist understandings of the church are premised on the assumption that those joining the church are voluntarily, seriously, and joyously committing themselves to a life of following Jesus in the company of (and in accountability to) others on the path toward God, so church-related institutions must be premised on the assumption that those within them are voluntarily, seriously and joyously committed to following Jesus—in their corporate, institutional, life—and that they desire to be accountable to one another. This is no small assumption and it raises an old problem about our theology of the church. Martin Luther in 1526 discussed a "believers church" vision, and identified the reasons he did not chose that path to reform the church.

> In short, if one had the kind of people and persons who wanted to be Christians in earnest, the rules and regulations would soon be ready. But as yet I neither can nor desire to begin such a congregation or assembly or to make rules for it. For I have not yet the people or persons for it, nor do I see many who want it.[3]

I have said that unless we can find ways to apply our Anabaptist theology more explicitly and comprehensively to our institutional life I feel we should simply confess that we have been barking up the wrong theological tree for almost 500 years and become Lutherans. Why? We have claimed, in critical dialogue with other Christian traditions, that Jesus offers us an ethic which we are called to live in the here and now. To the multitude of Christian ways to evade the call to follow Jesus in life, we have said "NO!" "We are called to live by the ethic of Jesus, and we can do it, not perfectly, and not on our own power, but we can do it by God's grace."

Closely connected, we have denied the central claim of "mainline" Christian social ethics that there is no *social* ethic in Jesus and that the task of the social ethicist is to construct almost from scratch a social ethic, utilizing at most a few basic principles, such as "love" (undefined concretely by Jesus).[4] We have insisted that Jesus does provide a *social* ethic—that is, an ethic applicable for the life of *groups* of people, not only for *individuals*.

These various claims imply, it seems to me, that our theological tradition *requires* us to view our institutions as different, as "signs of God's reign," in a way parallel to the way we view Christian individuals and congregations as such signs. We have, I think, painted ourselves into a corner. From an Anabaptist perspective, church-related institutions should be "signs" of how to be together institutionally which reflect our theological commitments and offer life-giving alternatives to those patterns in our culture's corporate life which are destructive.

Another reason for the importance of this test is related to the

---

[3]Martin Luther, in his preface to "The German Mass and Order of Service," *Luther's Works* [Volume 53], Ulrich S. Leupold [editor], Helmut T. Lehmann [general editor] (Philadelphia: Fortress Press, 1965), 64.

[4]Cf. chapter one of John Howard Yoder's, *The Politics of Jesus* 2d ed. (Grand Rapids, MI: Eerdmans, 1994).

credibility and authenticity of our social witness. When we are speaking to *institutions* of society our "prophetic" words lack credibility and power unless our own institutional life models (to some modest degree) what we are calling other institutions to live by. If in our institutional life we do not live by (or even espouse) different standards than those we criticize in the world's institutions, we have no moral right to call them to repentance. In short, the test we face in applying our theology and ethics to our institutional life is not only a test of the integrity and workability of our convictions but also of the credibility of our social witness.

The Ethic of Jesus I have spoken so far as if "the ethic of Jesus" was something self-evident. Of course, it is not.[5] I am surely not in a position to outline it, using the tools of biblical scholarship. What I wish to do here is more modest: to highlight aspects of the ethic of Jesus which, first, those in the Anabaptist tradition have highlighted and, second, appear to be pertinent to issues faced by institutional administrators.

Leadership. In Jesus we have "the first shall be last," servanthood, not lording over, the master image of Jesus the messiah, the King, dying on the cross. We have a blessing of the meek. The contrast is sharp with prevailing images of kings, leaders as those in control, strong, in charge.

Structure. We have seen Jesus as calling into being a community, a priesthood of all believers, in which we are not superiors and inferiors, but brothers and sisters. This clearly stands in sharp tension with normal, hierarchical, pyramidal, institutional structures.

Decision making. We have stressed decision making by community discernment and consensus, focused around the Bible, and listening to the Spirit ("it has seemed good to the Holy Spirit and to us"). We have seen this as standing in contrast to common patterns of institutional decision making where a decision is made at the top by the boss, and where it appears that rational debate and power-moves figure far more predominantly in decisions than does the Bible or listening for the Spirit's voice.

Power. We have believed that Christ calls us to a power that invites but does not compel others. We have heard the words, "take no thought

---

[5]What to make of this lack of self-evidence, from our modern, academic perspective, is another matter. Is it mainly that it is unclear, or that we look for ways to avoid seeing its clarity? I know for me it is some of both. It is worth noting, however, that arguments claiming Jesus is far less clear on these matters, than "we" in the Anabaptist tradition have thought he was, have been central to the case made against us from the beginning by our theological opponents standing in various "mainstreams."

for the morrow," words calling us to relinquish control of our futures and rest in God's providence. Again the contrast is sharp, since often in institutions power is seen as the ability to force others to do what they don't want to, the ability to dominate, the ability to not only think about but to insure our safety into the indefinite future,

Focus of attention. Our theology teaches us to attend to God, and to God in the least of these. There we see Jesus. The institutions of the world teach us to attend to those who are most important, the ones who carry the most prestige, weight, wealth, argumentative skill, to honour those who contribute much (in various ways) with banquets recognizing them, or with endowment funds or buildings named after them.

Norm. In Jesus we have modeled norms such as compassion, mercy, forgiveness, or justice defined as meeting needs. Prevailing understandings of justice in the institutions of our world, in contrast, revolve around notions like justice meaning payment for the value of services, the value of a person's skills in the marketplace. Thus it is "just" for top executives to receive millions of dollars annually while billions of the world's people eke out, or fail to eke out, a bare existence because they do not have skills (or positions) valued in the marketplace.

More contrasts could be added. But I hope I have said enough to show two things. First, there are some differences between views from our heritage which shape understandings of institutionally relevant matters and views frequently dominant in institutions of our culture. And second, there are some serious struggles to be faced by administrators who would like to run institutions that stand in our theological tradition. I have been close to enough good Anabaptist-Mennonite administrators to have no illusions that it is an easy task.

I would suggest that the most unique and most important challenge facing administrators in Mennonite educational institutions is this: demonstrating in "flesh," in the actuality of institutional life, the truth of the peculiar gospel we proclaim. Can we, in convincing, authentic ways, relate our faith to the realities of our institutional life? A positive answer to this question is necessary if we are to salvage the Anabaptist-Mennonite theological heritage which, ironically, significant numbers of people outside our circles are now attracted to, but which some of us, confronted with the realities of our institutional life, now seem to feel must be abandoned for more Lutheran, or Niebuhrian, perspectives.

How Mennonite Christian Faith Should Shape the Way We Operate Our Institutions I wish to highlight four "next steps" on the journey toward connecting more fully our theological-ethical convictions with our institutional life: focusing, imagining, committing, and worshipping,

Focusing. Perhaps the most critical issue before us is what we focus on, the lens we use to interpret reality, the window through which we "see" our world. "Reality" is not self-interpreting, and it makes all the difference how we train ourselves to "see" it.

I think it is not accidental that Jesus talks so much about seeing. One small example, from Matthew 11. Jesus tells John's disciples who want to know if he is the Messiah, "Go tell John what you *hear* and *see*; the blind receive their sight, the lame walk, the lepers are cleansed, the deaf hear, the dead are raised up, and the poor have good news preached to them." What Jesus *saw* was the healing, the restoring. And he instructed John's disciples to see, and to report, *that*. My inclination would have been to see what was going on in a very different way, to see that there were still many unhealed, that Jesus' work was only a drop in the bucket—if I would have "seen" any miraculous healing going on at all.

Nothing is more important for us than to develop the habit of "seeing" reality through the window of Jesus Christ. It does not come easily or automatically for us because there are many compelling ways to construe reality and we have all been educated, whether through formal study in academic "disciplines" or through commercials on television, to see reality in different, often competing, ways. To train ourselves to see reality through the window of Jesus Christ will likely take as much time, energy and "discipline" as it takes those of us who are academics to learn, and practice, our academic disciplines. For administrators I surely think it will require intentional quiet time, listening, seeing, focusing.

I do not mean that we should refuse to look through other windows that can illuminate reality. We need many windows. But I do mean that an essential part of being *Christian* is cultivating habits of heart and mind which cause us to see reality first through the window of Jesus Christ, so that we come to see the world more and more in the way that Christ sees it. I do mean that the vision we get by looking through all other windows, must be tested and judged by the view of reality we see through the window of Jesus Christ, not vice versa. I do mean that it is never legitimate to simply ignore the window of Jesus Christ. Ignoring this window seldom happens through intention, but rather through habit and through our acclimatization to "the way things are done." Administrators are called to always direct our eyes to Jesus, to create a culture where it is as natural to look to him as it is to look at the college across the city or across the state.

Imagining. It is evident that focusing on Jesus Christ, even a "rethought" Jesus Christ, will not provide specific answers to most of the particular questions we face when we make institutional decisions. I do not think that this (frequent) lack of specificity for our situation means that our Lord is largely irrelevant to our decisions, however. What we need rather is imagination, an imagination tuned to him.

God's gift of the human, historical Jesus is at this point complemented and completed by the gift of the Spirit, a Spirit which, Jesus promises, "will guide you into all the truth" (John 16:13). We know that this truth will be consistent with Jesus, (a "truth" inconsistent with Jesus is not a Christian truth) but that more will be shown to us than was shown to us in Jesus' earthly life (cf., John 16:12ff). Finding the specific truth we need for our institutions in our context requires of us openness to the Spirit as we are led to imagine new things, new ways of being saintly institutions.

I suspect that the Spirit's most important work in enabling us to create more saintly institutions is to free our imaginations from bondage to the "legalisms" of what our age, and some of our academic disciplines, "know" about how institutions "must" be.[6] God's grace sets us free from assumptions about institutional patterns that hurt others and us. We can dare to imagine, and to implement alternatives.

Obviously, I do not have detailed proposals for what all those alternatives might be. But I believe there are many creative possibilities, and certainly many areas in which alternatives are needed if we are to connect our faith to our institutional life more coherently and winsomely. I think of areas such as: hiring and firing; use of power; decision making procedures and the conduct of meetings; structures; leadership and accountability; fund raising; constituency, board and staff relations—the list could go on. But to avoid leaving all this at a completely abstract and theoretical level, let me share some brainstorms.[7]

As a sign of our oneness in Christ and as an act of mutual aid within our worldwide Anabaptist family of faith, our North American church-related institutions adopt a policy of giving one percent of their annual budgets to sister institutions in the "two thirds" world. A policy such as this would, it seems to me, embody in a small way the spirit of practical care for one another reflected in the offerings St. Paul collected for the needy church in Jerusalem.

I have ambivalence about this. On the one hand, I have seen heads wag and knowing smiles appear when similar proposals are made, clear signs that such an idea is seen as radically impossible, "unrealistic." On the other hand, I remember the gentle, joking, and yet telling response

---

[6]I am grateful to Alan Kreider for suggesting this way to think about "legalism."

[7]In thinking about economic implications of Christian faith I find helpful Perry B. Yoder's comparison of the "economics of shalom" and the "economics of wealth." See his *Shalom: The Bible's Word for Salvation, Justice, and Peace* (Newton, KS: Faith and Life Press, 1987), 111-112.

from a Colombian Mennonite when in conversation I made a similar suggestion: "Isn't the biblical standard ten percent?"

Compensation policy. I have been disturbed by the trend in the church-related institutions I know toward adopting revised compensation patterns that increase gaps between those highest paid and those lowest paid because I cannot see how such patterns embody Jesus' care for the marginalized, the concern for equality which marked the early church, or how they can empower a prophetic witness to the institutions of our society in favour of compassionate and (biblically-defined) "just" economic policies. I have also been disturbed by a move to adopt parity with similar institutions as the explicit criterion for determining compensation levels because it suggests to me that Jesus and our understanding of our faith are not seen as normative, or even relevant, for setting salaries. I do not see how we could object, on the basis of the compensation principle we ourselves advocate, if General Motors pays its chief executive fifteen million dollars a year if Ford pays equivalently, since they are similar institutions.

Imagine these principles serving as the basis for determining compensation.

A "living wage." Should be paid to all those whose time is given to the institution since employment here prevents other substantial earnings. The idea is that all those working in our institutions full time should be paid enough to provide a minimally decent living for themselves and their families. This living wage could be determined for various family sizes by using standardized measures of the cost of living in various locations, such as the local poverty line, and then multiplying that by some agreed number.

Wages should include increments for investment in preparation required for the job and for job demands. Treating people equally economically requires that years spent obtaining education needed for the job be compensated, since otherwise those years could have been income producing years. In addition, some jobs are far more demanding in terms of hours and/or in terms of stress, leaving less time and energy for other activities, whether for supplemental earnings or expense reduction (like doing one's own house repairs), or for pursuing personal interests.

Meeting needs. Central to the "shalom" of the community and to the vision of the church in the New Testament is that there be no needy among us (Acts 4:34-35), that there be "equality" (2 Corinthians 8:14; KJV, RSV) or a "fair balance" (NRSV). I suggest that this "need" component of salaries include a policy through which 1 percent (say) of salaries is put into a "mutual aid fund" which a committee would administer to meet exceptional needs of employees and their families. My vision here also includes setting "target" incomes for families of various sizes (these targets being what "desirable" incomes for various families would be, not minimal living wages), and adjusting the salaries of church institutional employees to bring their total family incomes toward those targets, thus reducing the gap between rich and poor in our own institutions.[8]

On these and many other matters of administrative policies I don't have answers. But I am confident that as we look at our institutional life more and more focusedly through the window of Jesus Christ, using the gift of imaginations directed by the Spirit, we will find alternatives that will bring our institutional lives closer and closer to our theological-ethical vision.

Committing. There is another step needed, one which no Anabaptist theology can ignore: committing. It is this issue of commitment that is my deepest reason for worrying about the feasibility of the Anabaptist conception of faith and life. Do we, unlike those Luther saw around him, want to be "Christians in earnest"? Or are Luther's reasons for rejecting a "believers' church" alternative valid? Was he right, after all?

Even when administrators are open to patterns which are more reflective (in my judgment) of our Anabaptist Christian convictions and may have ideas about what such patterns are, often those of us within their organizations resist them. Often administrators would like to be more radical than we allow them to be, insisting as we do on our "rights," comparing ourselves always to those better off than we are. Are we who work in and support our schools committed to "saintliness"? I wonder, and I worry.

Worshipping. Despite the centrality of commitment in Anabaptist understandings of faith, it is surely the case that simply having administrators tell us to grit our teeth and deepen our commitment will not enable more saintly living, either personally or institutionally. Perhaps the biggest challenge facing administrators is to find ways of articulating a vision for saintly institutions which is winsome, inviting, and exciting, not to whip up "commitment." Perhaps the single most important quality of leaders for our institutions is ability to "see" Jesus Christ clearly and imaginatively and to communicate what is seen winsomely. For while following Jesus Christ is often hard work, even dangerous, to follow him is to walk the path to life, to joy. This brings us around to worship, for it is in worship that we see Jesus Christ.

I increasingly believe that worship is and must be at the centre of a Mennonite institution. And I am coming to believe that in our schools

---

[8]Additional detail on how this might work is included in my essay "Church-Related Institutions: Signs of God's Reign?" *Mennonite Quarterly Review* (July 1997): 433-437.

we need contexts in which the faculty and staff worship together without students, as well as doing business together. Such times of worship by those charged with the ongoing nurture of students could become critical times for focusing afresh on mission and identity. They could be times of prayer together, and for one another and for our students. They could be times of communion and footwashing, times of confession and of forgiveness. They could provide opportunities for wounds to be dealt with and healed. Perhaps they could be a bit like some older modes of Mennonite communion—times for self-examination, times to speak to one another whatever words are needed for reconciliation, times for words of love and affirmation. It is so easy (perhaps especially in our schools and other institutions) not to say both the hard things (confessing sins or hurts) and the deep caring things. Creating sacred spaces and times for such interactions within the symbolic framework of the faith could, I believe, deeply enrich life within our schools.

Worship should, of course, extend beyond faculty and staff. It is in worship that our hearts are prepared to respond, freely, joyfully, to the invitation to saintly living. It is in worship that we are most apt to see our lives truly—as undeserved grace from God's hand. Worship, I think, must have a central place in church institutions, because the grateful posture that comes through worship undergirds all saintly living. It can move us beyond a hang-up on rights, fairness, to a focus on grace, gift. There can be no doubt, of course, that efforts should be made by administrators to develop and implement fair policies and procedures. Yet somehow an ethos in which "fairness" is the highest norm seems self-destructive. When we focus on what we deserve, and compare ourselves to others, we will almost always feel cheated, slighted, treated unfairly. Our spirits will become narrow, bitter. To create an ethos, and an institutional culture, in which people experience grace and treat each other with grace—this is another central challenge of administrators and one that can be addressed by strengthening our worship.

What I Want from Administrators, and What I Want to Give Them In this section I want to share an attitude, a posture, that I hope would characterize relationships between administrators and other employees at our schools.

When my "boss," friend, and intellectual companion, Associated Mennonite Biblical Seminary President Marlin Miller, died suddenly in 1993 and my wife Gayle was thrust into the role of Acting President I found myself asking questions such as these: "What can we learn from this tragedy? What are the things I regret about how I related to Marlin? What are the things I am grateful for? What do I expect from, need from, primary administrators? And, especially, what do I pledge to give to them, what do I owe them?"

My reflections on these questions are coloured by my friendship with Marlin and the pain of his loss. They are coloured by my vantage point as spouse of a major administrator—Gayle was Dean at AMBS before becoming Acting President. They also reflect my own position at AMBS: something of a "mid-level" employee—not an administrator, and not a "support staff" member, but a professor. But despite their limits, I hope they may stimulate prayerful thought about relationships between leaders and followers.

I have come to feel that what we need most in our institutional life is a covenant between administrators and employees—a covenant of love. It cannot be a contract. Perhaps a "covenant of love" sounds too intimate, but I do not mean it to suggest mainly a warm sentiment or even, necessarily, a close personal relationship. I mean rather a deep care for the well being of the other, a care that enables the other to carry out his or her tasks with energy and joy.

As I have reflected on this covenant of love one thing that I have asked myself is, "What do I need from my administrators?"

I need my supervisor's *blessing* in my vocation. I do what I do out of a sense of calling. I need to know that my supervisor believes my being here is a right response to my calling. I need affirmation, encouragement. I need to be told what I do right, not only what I do wrong.

I need *honest communication*. I *do* need to be told what I do wrong. I need straight, clear, and loving feedback on my failings—and on my future with the institution. I need to be told if others do not see me as suited for, called to, my role. I also want to know the state of the institution and its future. My life is bound up with it.

I need a *sense of participation* in, ownership of, the enterprise to which I am giving my life's energies. I need the opportunity to speak on issues that affect me personally. I also need a voice on larger matters of institutional direction. I want my administrators to be approachable, through formal channels and informally.

I need *leadership and decision-making*, not only facilitation. I need administrators who will take the risk and responsibility of leading, people who listen not only to the various human voices around them but to God's voice and then propose courses of action based on that listening. This does not mean I want autocratic leaders. Before decisions are made I need clarity about where and how they will be made and how I can have input in them if I want to. But the burden of leadership is responsibility to lead.

I need *respect*. I mean this generally, but in a specific sense also. I need administrators who assume that I care about our mission, that I want the good of the whole, that when I speak I speak out concern for our mission. I want them to see me as one who cares passionately about our future, and not only as a member of a "pressure group" representing a set of "interests."

Although my administrators have sometimes failed to give me all of what I need from them, I am grateful for how well they have done in blessing me. Reflecting on these matters has humbled and grieved me, however. I have seen more clearly the ways in which I have failed to give them what I believe I owe them in a "covenant of love." Leadership in church institutions is often not an easy task. And too frequently people who work in those institutions make it difficult—*I* make it difficult. And so I desire to make, and to live out, the following pledges to my administrators.

I pledge to give a *blessing*. I desire to remember you daily in prayer. I desire to check in with you regularly. I intend to speak some specific word of encouragement to you at least monthly, either orally or in writing. I want you to know that I value the life's energy you are giving to my institution, and that I pray routinely for the blessing of God to be evident in your work and life. I pray that your work will be life giving to you, not draining. I promise to cultivate a spirit in me that sees you as one of God's good gifts to me. As I look back on my relationship with Marlin, nothing gives me greater pain than remembering those times when I forgot to pray for him or when I knew him weighed down by a hard matter and did not communicate my care to him. And nothing eases the pain of his loss more than remembering those times when I did communicate "blessing" to him from the heart. I have come to see praying for "those in authority" over me in a new light.

I pledge to give *honest feedback*. I know that you may be left in the dark, unaware of what employees are thinking, saying. I desire to avoid letting things build up inside me so that a silent, invisible barrier prevents communication. I pledge to speak up when I am disturbed about something or when I see you becoming weighed down—seeking to remember at the same time that you are busy. I do not want to burden you with every little problem or idea. I pledge to seek to discern what is important to say and what is not.

I pledge to *respect your charge* to shape the overall direction of our life together and our mission. I confess that it is easy for me to assume that I see things more clearly than you do. I seek to respect your mandate to lead. I will try to remember that when you disagree with my "wisdom" it is not necessarily because you have not listened to me—it may mean that you have listened to me *and* to others who disagree with me. I will keep in mind the saying, "Where you stand depends upon where you sit." I will try to remember that your "seat" usually gives you a better vantage point for making judgments about our overall life together than does my "seat" and to give you the benefit of the doubt.

I pledge to you a *spirit of teamwork.* I have noticed how easy it is for an adversarial assumption to creep into our relationship. Because you have larger overall responsibility, you also have more power. It is easy for me to feel resentful of that, easy to feel ignored, unappreciated, unheard, sometimes even exploited. It is easy for me to develop a "we-they" mentality in which *you* become the opponent. It is easy for me to see everything as a power contest and to dismiss the views of others cynically as representing their "interests." Perspectives such as these do more to undermine the spirit of cooperation in an institution than anything else. I pledge to remind myself, again and again, that we are on the same team, working toward a common end.

My observation of Marlin and my life with Gayle have left me with other questions about what a covenant of love between the church and its administrators might look like. They are questions that are larger than my personal relationships with and attitudes toward administrators. They are questions for the wider church, and especially for boards which oversee primary administrators.

In a time of cutting back in many institutions, how do we avoid a work overload for top administrators? I know that AMBS kept telling Marlin to slow down. But we also kept telling him, "This needs doing, that needs doing." How can we avoid giving these double messages?

I also know that life for primary administrators is often lonely. It is routine that the hardest things that administrators face are things that cannot be shared in the circles they normally turn to for support. How do we provide administrators with personal, emotional, and spiritual support? And how do we make sure that there are at least a few people who know them well enough to help ease the burden, to notice when the weight is too much, to whom they can speak, and who can speak to them and be heard? Perhaps regular retreats, spiritual direction, and support groups can help. In any case confidants in addition to spouses are needed.

When Nelson Kraybill was inaugurated as AMBS President in March 1997, he was wrapped in a shawl that had woven into it the written prayers of many connected to the seminary. It was, I felt, a perfect symbol of what I suspect administrators need most from those whom they lead, supervise, and serve: our loving prayers on their behalf. When we offer prayers filled with love on behalf of those who lead us, we will find it easier to speak directly, to listen openly, and to respect their leadership. And when we are recipients of their prayers, they will speak to us in ways that are easier for us to hear, because they will speak to us out of love.

Conclusion: Sharing the Blessing Why do we have Mennonite educational institutions? I would say that we have them in order to share the blessing which has come to us through our Mennonite

Christian faith, to pass it on, to invite others to discover the joy of knowing God's love in Jesus Christ, and responding in love to it.

Sharing the blessing! I am awed, fearful, yet so grateful, when I call to mind God's promise to Abram and Sarah, the promise that "I will bless you," and "by you all the families of the earth will be blessed," and how that blessing has been passed down to my generation by an unbroken chain of saints. I am awed by those saints, and by God. I am grateful because of what that faith means to me—life. Yet I am fearful because it seems to me an awesome thing to stand at the end, for now, of that chain of blessing, and to know that the faith of the next generation is in our hands, after having been passed on to us at such cost. I do not want to be the link that breaks the chain of blessing.

Administrators of our schools bear a special responsibility to shape their institutions so that they are fit instruments for passing on the blessing to the next generation. It can feel like a heavy burden, seeing the pictures of past presidents who have passed on the faith and the institution, knowing the sacrifices of past generations and of the present generation, knowing that the shaping of the faith of the next generation is significant, not trivial, in the work of God's reign on earth. Administrators in our schools are important links in the chain of blessing. To a large degree, on them rides the question of whether our schools will go the route of secularization followed by so many schools started by churches in North America. I will not minimize the weight of responsibility which administrators carry for passing on the blessing.

To be a fit custodian of the institutions of blessing that our schools are called to be, administrators need attentiveness to the inner life of the spirit. Some time ago I found myself writing these words to a friend who had become a leader in one of our church-related institutions. They speak to the themes of blessing, and the inner walk.

> While you know I have celebrated your choice for this role, I have also sensed the loss of what might have come from that more intense inward journey you might have taken. You surely must guard against giving that inward journey up entirely. For it is, I expect, people's sense of a deep inward journey in you (along with your obvious public gifts) that led to the excitement which many of us felt when we learned of your appointment. And without it the key intangible qualities that are so essential to the kind of leadership you want to provide will gradually, imperceptibly, fade. Even in the midst of your very public life, you know better than I that some balance must be maintained, however difficult it might be to do.
>
> In our conversation I spoke of the chain of blessing that has come down to us, and of our responsibility to pass the blessing on. As I write I look out of my window onto the Elkhart River, sun glinting constantly yet everchangingly. It reminds me that God's blessing and the blessing of faith in Jesus Christ are not only, not mainly, like a chain. Rather they are like a stream, flowing on, from Abram and Sarah to us—and, of course, past us,

out of sight, just as the river bends and passes from my sight, but does not stop flowing. You have a unique opportunity, and responsibility, to help pass on the blessing in your role. Yet, more important (this is of course not news to you!), you float on that stream of blessing. You do not carry the blessing; it carries you. And its flowing does not depend on you. You couldn't stop it if you wanted to; it would wash over and around you, flowing on. So . . . on the one hand, much is given to and required of you . . . and on the other hand, little really depends on you. The river is God's. Your main job is to float on that stream of blessing, enjoying the ride, letting it carry you, inviting others to jump in and float along. How's that for a job description?!

My prayer for you who are administrators of our schools is that you may help make our schools inviting places where many, for generations to come, as in generations past, take the plunge into the river of God's blessing—that small, but precious, river of blessing that we know as Mennonite Christian faith. And that in doing so, you yourselves have a great ride![9]

---

[9]Substantial portions of this essay have appeared previously in *Mennonite Quarterly Review* (July 1997) and in *Gospel Herald* (April 23, 1996).

9 The Invisible Curriculum—On Being Wisdom's School

Thomas R. Yoder Neufeld[1]

Introduction "The Invisible Curriculum" is somewhat of an "invisible topic." *"Hidden* curriculum" does enjoy considerable currency in the literature, but it usually carries overtones of pedagogical and political deviousness, surely not the topic on this occasion. "Invisible" might also be taken to refer to the *extra*-curricular elements of an educational experience, such as residence, chapel, or the athletic programs. These represent, however, some of the most *visible* dimensions of our educational institutions, as is amply demonstrated whenever students rehearse what has been most important to them during their sojourn at one of our schools. What is, in my view, most "invisible," and at the same time most determinative of the overall effect of our institutions, is the ethos, the ambience, the environment, what and how we teach in intended and unintended ways via our "life-style," individually and collectively. Here we have to do with such invisible matters as vision, motivation, integrity, and spirituality—of individuals and of institutions. It is this slippery something the organizers of this conference were after most especially.

By the very nature of things it is impossible to establish the contours and edges of the invisible. As all know too well, we are not our students' only teachers, their only school. We exist alongside the schools and teachers of church, family, friends, and a myriad of cultural and social forces.[2] If that is true with respect to our "visible" teaching,

---

[1]Associate Professor of Religious Studies and Peace and Conflict Studies, Conrad Grebel College.

[2]As Don Kraybill reminded us already twenty years ago; *Mennonite Education* (Scottdale, PA: Herald, 1978), 16.

it is doubly true of our invisible curriculum. However humble we might be about our own importance as educators, we all know intuitively that we are engaged in an educational enterprise that includes that invisible "extra" we are here calling the invisible curriculum. Each of us, depending on our disciplines, our role within our school, on the particular species of Mennonite school we come from, most importantly on our vision of the Christian life, will have a different take on what this invisible curriculum is and what it should be. I will engage the topic as a teacher of Bible at a Mennonite school which, unlike many of the schools represented here, is perched on a fence shared and paid for by both church and university. Let me share with you what I see from that rather limited and sometimes uncomfortable perch. I do so with the assumption that I see some things you can see as well from where you sit.

The Wisdom Tradition   I want to begin by drawing attention to a strain of biblical tradition which is particularly relevant to our topic—relevant not because we pay much attention to it in the Menno-nite community but because we should. It is among us the most invisible of traditions, the tradition of wisdom.[3]

Why is the wisdom tradition relevant? First, because it is the biblical tradition most immediately and obviously related to the task of education. As a perusal of wisdom writings from Proverbs to Psalms, from the Song of Solomon to the Wisdom of Solomon, from Ecclesias-tes to Ecclesiasticus illustrates richly, it is in Israel's wisdom that we discover the range and depth of interest Israel's educators had in creation, in history, in social and political dynamics, in literature and poetry, in the sublimely spiritual and the sublimely physical, and in the way the divine will is reflected in both the predictable and unpredictable dimensions of human life. These inquisitive sages were for all that no less interested in the earthy, personal, and political practicalities of

---

[3]I was heartened to find several fine Mennonite contributions to our educational musings that draw heavily on the wisdom tradition, one a sermon by Patty Shelly at a previous consultation on Mennonite Higher Education entitled "Wonder and Worship," *Mennonite Higher Education: Experience and Vision: A Symposium on Mennonite Higher Education*, edited by Ken Hawkley (Bluffton College, 1992), 181-186; the other a delightfully insightful piece by Delbert Wiens, "The Christian College as Heresy," in *Mennonite Idealism and Higher Education: The Story of the Fresno Pacific College Idea*, edited by Paul Toews (Fresno, CA: Center for Mennonite Brethren Studies, 1995), 43-65. See also Charles F. Melchert, "Wisdom is Vindicated By Her Deeds," *Religious Education* 87/1 (1992): 127-151.

living in light of such wisdom, in knowing how to act and when to act, what to say, and when to say it—or, just as often, when to hold one's most lethal and dangerous organ, the tongue. In their view, to live is to be in school—to be engaged in a permanent process of learning and formation, of developing habits of mind, heart, and body so as to skilfully navigate the voyage of life. Israel's sages attempted to understand the will of God as embodied both in Torah and broad human experience so as to live right, which is to say, righteously. Remarkably, their attentiveness to wisdom often took them beyond the confines of their own communities and traditions, believing as they did that God's wisdom informs *all* of creation, and can therefore be encountered profitably in the courts and stoas of other peoples. And finally, as happened all too often, when sages experienced life as incomprehensible tragedy, their struggles to find meaning were expressed in an unsurpassed mix of analysis, accusation, and some-times acceptance or acquiescence. Even at such dark times they found the resources to put that tormented struggle into poetry, as we see in Job.

As this all-too-hasty sketch of the wisdom tradition makes clear, there is no dimension of learning at any of the various Mennonite schools that is beyond wisdom's curriculum, whether we have in mind the visible curricula of science, social science, literature, music, ethics, philosophy, theology, and biblical study, or the invisible curricula of institutional structures and procedures, community life, character formation, faith, worship, and play. We will thus choose to emphasize this or that in our curricula only for practical and strategic reasons, not because anything is beyond the pale for the devotees of divine wisdom.

Perhaps a more important point of relevance for our post-modern age is, secondly, that the wisdom tradition presents us with a holistic vision of knowledge and understanding. Torah, science, worship, ethics, joyful appreciation of the varied gifts of life and tormented struggle with its vicissitudes—all *together* constitute an indivisible whole to be experienced and lived out in the presence of the one God whose wisdom at work in creation is the same as that bringing about salvation. This is quite unlike the contemporary tendency toward abstraction and distinction—toward *hairesis* (the post-modern heresy?).[4] Even within

---

[4]See the above mentioned article by Delbert Wiens. See also the clear-eyed critique of contextualism run amok by Max L. Stackhouse, *Apologia: Contextualization, Globalization, and Mission in Theological Education* (Grand Rapids, MI: Eerdmans, 1988), 22 and *passim*.

a self-consciously distinct *hairesis* such as the Mennonite community, we draw distinctions between theologies, disciplines, and between kinds of schools.

With respect to the wisdom tradition specifically, I find a special irony in how scholars dissect the wisdom literature, searching for genres, provenances, and species of wisdom. Whatever the payoff of such taxonomical compulsiveness might be—and it is quite considerable—it easily obscures the genius of Israel's sages. After all, these distinctions and abstractions must be extracted from a wonderfully holistic "Borscht" of experiential wisdom, riddles and aphorisms, philosophical ruminations, and not least poetic representations of the alluring figure of Sophia, to call Woman Wisdom by her Greek name. In her science, poetry, theology, and worship cohere. In her love and justice embrace. In her the love of God becomes pleasure. Sophia is there at creation as God's daughter and architect of creation (Prov. 8:22-31), and is therefore in a perfect position to be Solomon's science tutor (Wis. 7:15-22); God sends her to find a home among humanity, and she finds it in Jacob (Sirach 24); once there, on the hilltops and at the gates, she seduces Israel's youth, and most especially the insatiable Solomon, by throwing a party of bread and wine (Prov. 9). The party game, learning how to walk straight, or, as we are more used to putting it, the study of Torah (Prov. 8; Sirach 24; Baruch 3:9-4:4). This serious playfulness, this "godly mirth," to quote a phrase from one of Handel's Chandos Anthems, is captured wonderfully in the title of one of my favourite Beatles' songs off their famous White Album, *Dear Prudence, Won't You Come Out to Play?* To be sure, life with Sophia can also be dangerous; she is also a fearsome and glorious enforcer of God's will in both judgment and salvation (e.g., Wis. 10-18).

In Sophia we encounter a vision of wholeness, of perfection, a paradigm of education in which our curricular concerns are only one part of a larger enterprise in which ambience, atmosphere, and style are as essential as specific impartation of information: an ethos in which creation in all its fullness is embraced as Wisdom's craft; an atmosphere in which the love of Wisdom is indistinguishable from the love of God; in which the pursuit of insight is inseparable from the exercise of prudence; an ambience in which learning is inseparable from worship, and in which worship finds its greatest creative expression in a life well and righteously lived—loving God with all of one's heart, mind, soul, and strength. There is thus room in Wisdom's home for us all: technofiles and theologians, poets and painters, athletes and administrators—a home in the presence of God. Here is a vision at odds with the academic habits of dispassionate analysis, cool observation, and cold control.

Christ, the Wisdom of God This would be enough grist for our mill were it not for one more dimension of this biblical tradition, the most important one for Christians, and one particularly relevant to the Mennonite educational enterprise. As stated earlier, Israel's wisdom tradition was an amalgam of Torah reflection and adaptation of the wisdom of the world; it represented intense reflection on the very particular gift of God to Israel in the Torah, but doing so with an ear to the ground and its face to the world—to mix metaphors. For that reason the traditions of wisdom constituted the deepest and richest well from which early followers of Jesus drew in giving expression to his significance for them and their world. While the largely royal "*Christos*" became the principal title with which Jesus' followers signalled their boundless respect for him, they parsed that royal designation largely by means of the categories of wisdom. The evangelists depict him as teacher par excellence, as a purveyor of practical wisdom, however subversive.[5] They describe his life as that of a righteous servant of God, who refuses to be compromised in the exercise of justice, at the predictable cost of his own life—a familiar wisdom scenario of what happens to those who do the right thing to the first bitter and then glorious end (cf., Isa. 53, Wis. 2-5, Phil. 2, and the Passion narratives in the Gospels). More important still, Jesus is depicted variously by Paul, Matthew, James, and John as God's *Sophia*, as *Logos* in the flesh, as Torah incarnate, as enabling, indwelling, and enthusing Spirit. Not surprisingly, this comes to poetic expression in the great wisdom hymns of John 1, Colossians 1, and Philippians 2. The marginalized and suffering Wisdom (1 Cor. 1:18-25; 2:7-8) is that very same Wisdom that fashioned "all things" (John 1:3; Col. 1:16), the Wisdom in and through whom are "all things gathered up" in an act of saving re-creation (Eph. 1:10; 2:11-22). Sophia is none other than the Logos who was already there at creation; he is Sophia having found a home with humanity, throwing a party of bread and

---

[5]See the recent work of, e.g., J. Dominic Crossan, *The Historical Jesus: The Life of a Mediterranean Jewish Peasant* (San Francisco: HarperCollins, 1991); and his *Jesus: A Revolutionary Biography* (San Francisco: HarperSanFrancisco, 1994); Burton Mack, *The Lost Gospel: The Book of Q and Christian Origins* (Philadelphia: Fortress, 1993); Ben Witherington, *Jesus the Sage: The Pilgrimage of Wisdom* (Minneapolis: Fortress, 1994). While some of the above focus on Jesus as sage to the point of serious distortion, it is an assured finding in all contemporary Jesus research.

wine (Matt. 11:19; Luke 7:35; cf., John 4, 6); he is Torah lived and taught (Matt. 5-7). "Where two or three are gathered in his name" there is co-habitation with Sophia (Matt. 18:20). To be "in Christ," the power and the wisdom of God (1 Cor. 1:24), is to have the Spirit of Sophia pulsing through one's veins (to restate only slightly the gist of Paul's argument in Rom. 8, 2 Cor. 3, and Gal. 3).

This identification of Jesus not only as the Christ, but as the Wisdom of God, constitutes the most important point of Wisdom's relevance for us educators within the "following-Jesus" tradition, and this for two complementary reasons: first, it invites us to see Jesus and all he signifies in light of the full dimensions of biblical Wisdom. To put it differently, the account of those who introduced Jesus to us in the New Testament makes little if any sense outside of a full appreciation of Jewish wisdom. Conversely, and just as importantly, the identification of Jesus as Wisdom invites us to see Sophia and all she signifies in the light of her concretization in Jesus the Christ. To divorce Jesus from the usual concerns of the sages—"normal life" (individual *and* collective) within God's creation—misses one of the most critical implications of christology's birthplace in wisdom. The wisdom tradition, most especially as it relates to Jesus, urges on us a search for wisdom and insight that can never be undertaken faithfully apart from the story, the work, the teaching, and the saving significance of Jesus the crucified and risen Lord. Both our visible and invisible curricula, however diverse, however contextual, must serve this vision if we are to be the schools not simply of Menno's offspring, but of Sophia-Christos, who desires "in every generation to enter holy souls and to make them friends of God and prophets" (Wis. 7:27).

Wisdom and Mennonite Schools Let me now turn the light of this wisdom on ourselves as representing the Mennonite higher education community. First, a note of gratitude. To a significant degree, we are already Wisdom's school. Our institutions are blessed with skilled and informed scribes and sages, who publish and teach as well as anyone; our students are easily among the best and brightest, and most often become productive citizens; our institutions are run with efficiency, skill, and honesty by gifted administrators. In short, our supporting constituencies have every reason to be proud of our accomplishments. Students emerge from our schools skilled at navigating life professionally and academically. They are forging life-long bonds with fellow students. Having imbibed the wisdom of our tradition and a good deal of the wisdom of our world, many of them discover and appropriate a life-long faith which is creative, resilient, and practical; many are catching the vision of service; some respond with energy and joy to Christ's call to a life of ministry. These are great accomplishments for which we give God thanks.

> I know your works—your love, faith, service, and patient endurance. I know that your last works are greater than the first. But I have this against you . . . (Rev 2:19-20).

I also see many students whose relationship to God is at best tepid. Missing for many is a sense of how their life skills relate to the worship of God, how faith and knowledge, knowledge and practice relate. Their education is thus lacking the most essential element of divine wisdom. Many of them have either lost or never had a love for Scripture. Too often they have seen the Bible used by their peers and their mentors so selectively that it serves as little more than a legitimation for certain Mennonite core values or stances; the rest is uninteresting or irrelevant. Or the Bible has come to be viewed chiefly as a problem, as an impediment to human aspirations, rather than as a holy resource, let alone divine revelation. Our students increasingly ignore the Bible with impunity. And they are learning this in our schools. Such biblical and theological illiteracy leads then often, not surprisingly, to a seriously impoverished view of Jesus, who becomes little more than a VSer on permanent assignment, and thus a model for the few months or years in which our students will do the same before taking up a "real life." In my experience such a truncated christology is characteristic not of the "strangers and sojourners" among us, but of many Mennonite students who have come through our own educational system. They are increasingly unable to relate Jesus to the big picture, and thus find themselves unable to connect faith to science, to literature, to art, to the Jewish roots of our tradition, or, for that matter, to the great gospel of the Church and its central affirmations. To what extent do they learn this from teachers who are themselves incapable of making these connections in thought and life?

Some of our students arrive with an innocent evangelical zeal which we often see not as evidence of love for Sophia-Christos, one to be nurtured and deepened, so much as a fly in the Mennonite ointment (to adapt the Preacher's aphorism in Eccles. 10:1). Such students emerge from our schools either alienated from a Mennonite tradition they experience as inhospitable to them, leaving for the warmer climes of more conservative Christianity, or, having lost their first love, settle for the cool, distant relationship of looking on God's wisdom from afar, if they do not turn their back on her completely.

Many of our students are thus unable to give an account of their faith, much less give cogent and courageous witness. While learning that service and peacemaking are at the heart of Mennonite identity and ethos, they find evangelism and mission (in the more traditionally limited meaning) objectionable if not incomprehensible. They are left, ironically, notwithstanding all our globalization of education, with a truncated and parochial faith—a "softer faith," to recall Dale Schrag's characterization of some years ago.[6] It is a faith sustained chiefly by an ethnic glue to which, it turns out, just about anything adheres; for many of our students the bond of this glue is weakest with respect to the core convictions of a full-orbed biblical faith. Should we be surprised? They see among their mentors little if any search for new and appropriate ways of witnessing to God's wisdom in Christ—at least beyond the rather limited sphere of service and peacemaking—means and methods of evangelism rooted in a biblical message encompassing, but much bigger than, the Anabaptist tradition. Here the curricular silence at many of our schools reflects the invisible curriculum quite accurately.[7]

While many of our students see a brief interlude of service in their future, too many turn away from the costliness of being a humble lover of Wisdom-Christ, from servanthood as a mode of co-habitation with Wisdom, and choose instead power, privilege, and wealth. They do so with little discomfort. I see students far more able to relate to suffering

---

[6]"On First Commandments and Academic Heresies," in Ken Hawkley, ed., *Mennonite Higher Education*, 191. He quotes the striking comments of James Tunstead Burtchaell: "Religious faith comes forward nowadays in softer garments. Justice and peace, social service, awareness of and concern for the environment, volunteer work; or liberal arts, discriminating inquiry, courses in professional ethics, gender studies: these are presented as the contemporary surrogates for faith," in "The Decline and Fall of the Christian College [II]," *First Things* (May 1991): 36.

[7]I freely acknowledge that such an agenda is closer to the curricular commitments and the "invisible" intentions of some of our schools than to others. But this cannot remain the agenda of only a few among us. See Rodney J. Sawatsky's "Where in the World? Mennonite Colleges and Nonconformity," in Ken Hawkley, ed., *Mennonite Higher Education*, 79-95. See also John E. Toews, "The Church and Education in the Post-Modern Age," presented to the Mennonite Board of Education in 1994. He shares the concern expressed here. "The primary mission of church colleges will be to nurture the young people of the church into the faith and the church . . . . Training for professions and vocations is important, and will remain a task of the church colleges. But the primary mission . . . must shift to making the case for Christian faith and the church and to transmitting the faith to the young people of the church," 8-9.

abroad than to ordinary suffering folks next door, if they're fortunate enough to live next to ordinary folk—a fusion of globalism and domestic elitism. How does that get learned? Surely these too are the product of the ethos of our schools, not because we teach these things explicitly in our curricula—we don't—but because as their mentors we too have often opted for a cool faith and a safe distance.

Han can we shape the Invisible curriculum so as to become Wisdom's school? What would render our schools of higher learning more faithfully the classrooms in which Sophia is teacher, in which Christ is rabbi?

First, and here I can do no more than identify the issue, we need to render our whole educational enterprise more worshipful, more nurturing of the Spirit. I am not the first to say that; Patty Shelly expressed it profoundly some years ago in her sermon on "Wisdom and Worship" (*supra* n.2). If Sophia is to be our muse, if Christ is to be our fellow teacher, we must attend to that relationship more diligently. I sense a growing need in myself to see my colleagues and students as companions together in Wisdom's home, as friends of Jesus together. How we befriend each other as students, faculty, and administrators more deeply as brothers and sisters in Christ is often a delicate matter, given our resistance to the intimacies of faith. The quality of our invisible curriculum demands that we do, nonetheless. If, as Marlene Kropf proposed at a recent Ministers' Week at Conrad Grebel College, we should see church committee meetings as occasions of worship and pastoral care, surely we can find ways of "spiritualizing" the ambience of what eats up so much of our working days, whether committee meetings, council sessions, administrative and teaching chores, or day to day encounters with colleagues and students. All of this mix of creativity and tedium is both to be offered worshipfully to God as a gift and to be experienced as such. It is in this way that our spirits will be nourished—after all, it is in giving that we receive.

Second, for us to be Wisdom's school requires teachers who are, in addition to being expert scribes and scholars, on intimate terms with Christ, in love with Sophia, "inebriated by her fruits" (Sirach 1:16; cf., Eph. 5:18-20). We need to be teachers who experience both the pleasure and appreciate the holiness and gravity of their vocation, measured not only by their skills at communication and publication, but by their love for God, by the warmth and intimacy of their friendship with Christ. This is as critically important for those teaching science, music, and business as it is for those teaching theology and church history. I have long been sobered by the warning in that most sapiential of New Testament writings, the Letter of James: "Not many of you should become teachers, my brothers and sisters, for you know that we who teach will be judged with greater strictness" (3:1). As scholars, teachers, and mentors, we need to live our lives quite consciously in the presence of God, to see our work as joyful co-habitation with Sophia-Christos.

Such co-habitation does not and will not render us clones of each other. Nor will it stifle the generative creativity without which an academic environment suffocates—and, if my understanding of biblical wisdom is correct, without which a Christian environment suffocates. Sophia's lovers are many and diverse; Christ's circle of intimate friends is rich in variety. "The multivaried Sophia of God" (Eph. 3:10) requires a "multivaried" community of teachers.

Just as important, however, to be Wisdom's school necessitates that, with all our diversity of interests and styles as scholars and teachers, we *share* a home and a passion, that we celebrate our friendship with Christ in such a way that we experience each other as sisters and brothers, as true colleagues, and that our students thus see our project as essentially one. It is within such an ambience, such an ethos, that our students will be enticed into a life-long intimacy with Christ, with the capacity to give their own creative expression and witness to that relationship. Sophia will not abide voyeurs, nor will she tolerate those who stand at a safe and critical distance. Wisdom asks every teacher to take up her/his yoke, to enter her abode, or to let him into ours (Sirach 6:24; 51:26; Matt. 11:28-30; Rev. 3:20).

It is often observed that the pressures of scholarly performance have increased for Mennonite educators, pressures we embrace, for the most part. We communicate in many invisible ways to our students that it is promotion and advancement on the basis of professional criteria which constitute the true measure of a life worth having lived—regardless of what we teach on the explicit level. Times have changed sociologically from when teachers were pastors and priests. Ours is a different and more sophisticated world, and much of the change we observe in our academic environment is progress. Much of this is no doubt true. We may be better scholars, more sophisticated teachers. But surely that only renders more timely James' warning: "Let not many of you be teachers . . . ." It is exactly because of the changes in the direction of academic sophistication and accomplishment that it is the right time to ask ourselves as teachers whether we're in it for ourselves as individuals and as a guild, or whether we're in it for the sake of our friendship with Christ, our love of God, and all that implies for our relationship with colleagues and most especially students.

Third, the ethos of a school is, of course, only partly shaped by its teachers. We teach *within* an institution. But we also teach *through* and *as* an institution, however "invisibly." My sense is that it is at this structural, institutional, administrative level, that we find it most difficult to know how to allow the Wisdom that showed her face in Jesus to shape our life. Here we have largely ceded the field to the wisdom of Egypt, Babylon, or Greece—if you will. Our imaginations are in this respect Babylonian. We have been more acquisitive than transformative. There is of course much to be learned from Babylon—or Cambridge. But we forget that Babylon is our home but also the place of our captivity; we have become enamoured of its wisdom, and forget that we live in a strange land. And so we have little sense that we might have something to teach our world about what a school is, about what and who true wisdom is. We find, rather, safety in the models, structures, and relationships of management, accreditation, reward, and remuneration as they prevail in our wider culture.

True, we are not unaware of the tension between, on the one hand, the ideology or theology we identify as our raison d'être—the Anabaptist-Mennonite tradition of non-conformity which we teach at the explicit curricular level—and, on the other, the *modus operandi* of our institutions which does much to shape the invisible curriculum, which is smart, often wise, but it is hardly non-conformist.

Should it be? The answer we give, for the most part, is a clear if not particularly audible NO. And we do so largely with impunity because our supporting constituencies require of us that we are *not* non-conformist with respect to respectability, sound management, and full accreditation—as measured by criteria extraneous to our tradition. Most telling, *within* the walls of our schools there is a pervasive sense that one is safer with the structural, contractual, and remunerative common sense prevailing in the wider society than with something the church might cook up with its impractical recipe of servanthood, mutual care, and sacrificial service. Such churchly attempts are viewed by administrators and administrated alike as less just, less fair, and thus render faculty and staff vulnerable to injustice and abuse at the hands of administrators and boards, or, just as likely, administrators and boards at the hands of their employees. And so we seek ways to insulate ourselves institutionally against the way of life Jesus called for, a way of life we teach in our classes as the raison d'être of our tradition and the premise of our schools.

We have recently found a way to provide theological cover for ourselves by turning away from a recovery of vision to a recovery of the limits of vision, and a complementary but in my view specious retrieval of grace. I neither want to dismiss from the agenda and task of our sages reflection on the frailty and persistent sinfulness of human life, individually and corporately, nor, God forbid, on the divine gift of grace. But I am suspicious that in the process of marking out clearly the boundaries of perfection and holiness so that they do not encompass our institutions, all the while extending the boundaries of grace in such a way as to compensate for their exclusion, we are failing to heed the wisdom of that inspired sage who wrote the Letter to the Romans. After sketching in unforgettable strokes the boundless wonders of God's grace, Paul asks in 6:1 whether we should sin so that this grace might abound. It is *that* implied understanding of grace to which he gives a resounding NO. His clarion call in Romans 12 for non-conformity and, most importantly, for transformation of the mind and thus the habits of behaviour—individually *and* collectively/institutionally—grows out of his thoroughly Jewish conviction that such is the only fitting act of worship for those who have encountered the Wisdom of God in Christ. More, such worshipful and transforming nonconformity is a necessary precondition to knowing what is "good, and acceptable, and perfect"—as sapiential a list of the practical as one will find in the Bible, and as succinct a summary of what should be the heart of our curriculum, both visible and invisible. All this is *premised upon* the grace and mercy of God, celebrated in the immediately preceding verses as "the depth of the riches of the wisdom and knowledge of God" (Rom. 11:33-12:2).

Maybe Jesus did not "run anything," as one of our own sages has claimed; perhaps he was not "responsible for the founding and maintenance of a corporate organization."[8] But that that should render him less than immediately and critically relevant to the shaping and running of such institutions would have come as news to those who recognized in him the presence of that very Wisdom that fashioned creation, that sustains, nurtures, and instructs the human community in all—including collective and organized—dimensions of its life. The moment early followers of Jesus confessed him to be the Sophia of God they forever linked that teacher from rural Galilee to the courts of Jerusalem and Rome, and most assuredly to those institutions his followers would construct. That such a linkage would be forever troubled does not lessen its essential importance. In confessing Jesus to

---

[8]J. Lawrence Burkholder, "Autobiographical Reflections," in *The Limits of Perfection: A Conversation with J. Lawrence Burkholder*, edited by Rodney J. Sawatsky and Scott Holland (Kitchener, ON: Pandora Press, 1993), 19.

be Sophia his followers destabilized the value of common sense, and problematized our acquisition of such wisdom in the markets and lecture halls of this world. True, no doubt a school shaped by the Wisdom that is Christ will render us *more* vulnerable, *more* open to abuse, *more* fragile and *more* urgently in need of mutual trust. Trust by its very nature leaves one open to getting the short end of the stick. How could it be different if "the truth is in Jesus," as the inspired scribe puts it in Eph. 4:21? As in the case of Jesus, such vulnerable institutional faithfulness will constitute the way we will make a difference collectively, institutionally, the way we will participate in Wisdom's mending of our world.

I freely and humbly admit that I'm less sure than I should be about exactly how we enflesh, or rather "en-policy" a vision of God's wise and vulnerable reign; I am less sure than I am troubled by the impatience among us with the attempt, by the reluctance to try. I am heartened by Ted Koontz's call for "institutional saintliness."[9] I suspect, however, that his specific suggestions regarding a matter in which we are most likely to take refuge in the wisdom of this world—remuneration—will be met with less than enthusiasm. The criticism of his specific proposals is in my view less important than the ambience of our response. Do we object out of impatience to see Wisdom take shape institutionally? Does Koontz not go far enough? Or do we object that he is unrealistic about what works in our world? What would it mean to take up such a debate among us as sages impatient to see the Wisdom that is Christ find a home in Menno, a warm reception in our collective affairs, even if we do not agree quickly or easily on what that means practically? When our students see us at work, is this the impatience they learn, the air they breathe, the ethos they imbibe?

We will be faithful corporately and institutionally to the "wisdom from above" (James 3:17) only to the extent that as faculty, administrators, and boards we come to share the conviction that Wisdom resides in both most radical and most friendly (*Weltfreundlich*) fashion in Jesus the Christ. He was a radical subversive prophet who suffered at the hands of hostile humanity *not* because of his estrangement from human life, including its corporate institutional manifestations, but because of human resistance to God's will for human life. He went to

---

[9]"Church-Related Institutions: Signs of God's Reign," 3. Koontz has reiterated these concerns, see *supra*, chapter 8.

the cross because of having had too good a time eating and drinking with the wrong people, throwing Wisdom's joyful party for the "simple" (Matt 11; Prov 9). He got there too because of the institutional implications of his vision of human life as lived in the presence of God, expressed most dramatically in the prophetic demonstration in the temple. As his followers we should not bar him access to the boardrooms and councils of our schools, even were he to make a mess there. To follow Jesus, to name him Lord, to recognize him as the Sophia of God, is to confess that the wisdom he incarnates is God's Wisdom for this world, the Wisdom that pervades the structures of the cosmos, and not least the specific concretions of cosmos we know and live in, our institutions. "Blessed are those who do not take offence at him" (Matt. 11:6).

I conclude. Perhaps some of our students are quite untroubled in their pursuit of professional and monetary security by anything we have taught them regarding the radical wisdom of Jesus because we have not let it trouble us either. That would be sad. Perhaps some *are* troubled and then alarmed by the degree to which the radical heritage we pass on to them leaves us as teachers and institutions untroubled. That is good when it happens, even if uncomfortable for us. The worst and most damning effect of our own untroubledness, especially when alloyed with the rhetoric of radicalism, is if our students learn from us, visibly and invisibly, how to let our radical heritage serve as their ostensible raison d'être (what it means to be Anabaptist-Mennonite), but also how to manage it so as not to get in the way of the practicalities of existence. It is this luke-warmness which is in the eyes of God most distasteful (Rev. 3:15-16).

The sages of Israel and the church were enthusiastic borrowers precisely because they believed this to be in its entirety God's world, created through and with divine Wisdom. They borrowed most especially when it comes to the realm of institutional life. This can be seen in Proverbs, and no less in the patterns of organization and assembly we observe among early Christians. And we should not be ungrateful for what we ourselves have learned while in Egypt or Babylon—or Toronto. But those very same sages also warned against the allure of what Paul calls "the wisdom of this world" (1 Cor. 1:20), or James the wisdom that is "earthly and unspiritual" (3:15). It is characteristic of the wisdom tradition throughout its long and rich history to force the question of identity and faithfulness at precisely the point where "the wisdom from above" intersects with broad human experience and prevailing common sense. Our institutions of higher learning are located exactly at that intersection. For us who confess to being heirs of those who saw Wisdom appear in the flesh in Jesus the Christ, that intersection has been and must continue to be the critical testing ground of our fidelity. It is such fidelity which will render our invisible curriculum Wisdom's School.

----

10 The Invisible Curriculum II

Shirley Showalter[1]

Introduction I have brought with me two tools tonight. The first of those is memory. Memory allows me to revisit experiences of the past decade and of a life lived in school. Like many of you, I have been in school ever since I was six years old. There has never been a year when in some way or other I have not been attached to schooling purposes and where I have not been very aware of the fact that I love to learn and I love to teach. Ever since high school, I have been involved in Mennonite higher education, except for two years of public high school teaching and four years of classroom work in a major research university. Memories of a life lived in school, especially the joys and challenges of Mennonite higher education, are part of what I dwell on tonight.

Another tool that I bring with me is a method. I am adopting the method of Wisdom Woman who weaves together many threads, receiving impressions and recognizing that everything we study and everything that comes to us has a purpose from God. God has, indeed, created a magnificent universe. We can never stray outside God's universe, and our knowledge of it will never be greater than God's universe itself. Using memory and the method of Wisdom Woman, I want to weave strands of texts and ideas that have been important in my life together with strands of things that have happened during this conference.

One strand in my weaving must be the Renaissance. I did not anticipate that we would talk so much about that period of history, but

---

[1]President, Goshen College, Goshen, Indiana.

I think the Renaissance is both an exciting image and an exciting time period to help guide our thinking about the task that lies ahead for us as Mennonite educators. We were told that the Renaissance had four characteristics; it was local, particular, timely, and practical. I think these four characteristics match well where we have gone intuitively as a people throughout our history. I think we have had elements of the Renaissance with us all along, but those elements are being called forth in a particular time and a particular way in the present time.

Another strand that I bring to my weaving has not been mentioned during this conference, but it has shaped my own thinking, and it provides a counterpoint to the Enlightenment which the Renaissance humanist tradition made possible. That second strand is the monastic tradition. The monastic tradition, too, can help guide our thinking about Mennonite higher education that will be needed in the future. Jean LeClerq's book *The Love of Learning and the Desire for God* has been an important text for me. In it, LeClerq describes the medieval idea of the *lectio divina*, in which a text is consumed as though the Word of God were a sacrament that we could take into our bodies, and it would then come out in another form. I had an exactly opposite view of texts when I began my teaching career. I followed an encyclopedic model, trying to cram a long list of readings into every lecture so that students knew I was serious. The encyclopedic approach has its benefits; I certainly learned a great deal while I was making everybody else work very hard. Only over time did my teaching change, and I think that my spiritual life was just as important as my intellectual life in bringing about that change. The assignments I gave my students did not get easier, but they got less encyclopedic, because I began to appreciate what is possible if we digest a small meal carefully.

Texts I have chosen two texts for us to ponder in the *lectio divina* way. The first comes from the wisdom tradition that Tom alluded to earlier (see *supra* chapter 9). I was happy to learn about the wisdom tradition in the Bible because it explained to me why I love certain texts so much. Maybe your special texts are at different places in the Bible, but mine have always been those from the wisdom tradition. They stand out and speak directly to me. I didn't recognize that the things that I loved in Proverbs, like the story of creation in Proverbs 8 in which wisdom woman is with God from the very beginning, are linked to the New Testament wisdom hymns. One of those hymns is Colossians 1:15-17:

> He is the image of the invisible God, the first born over all creation. For by him all things were created; things in heaven and on earth, visible and

invisible, whether thrones or powers or rulers or authority, all things were created by him and for him. He is before all things, and in him all things hold together.

This wisdom hymn has been an important text for me all of this year. It was used in a litany during my inauguration ceremony at Goshen a few months ago. I have been living with it and trying to understand it. I know that my understanding is still incomplete, but I also know that I have been given that text.

The second text comes from St. Emily--Emily Dickinson that is. It is a brief part of a brief poem: "A word made flesh is seldom and tremblingly partook." Those are our texts to ponder.

Powerful Practices Let us move from these texts to a list of powerful practices that might help us think about what our institutions need--the faculty, students, staff, and the larger constituencies of alumni and church. Gerald Gerbrandt helped us imagine what we look like when you multiply out all of our constituencies. The sheer numbers of that collective group represent an impressive amount of energy, money, and dreaming. I hope that we go from this conference better prepared to lead within our own institutions, but also better prepared to lead a new denomination in discerning what education's role should and could be. What are some of the powerful practices that we can implement to help our students grow in wisdom? Here is a beginning list.

Connect with elders, saints, and wisdom figures. All of our institutions have wisdom resources that go beyond what we report to our accrediting agencies. This year's commencement speaker at Goshen College was George Gallup. He has written a book called *The Saints Among Us*, and so, in preparation for his coming, I read the book. I was amused first of all by the idea that a pollster could, in fact, define what a saint was. However, I began to think about the wisdom that he found by trying to look for people who really cared about being friends of God and whose whole lives are, in fact, testimonies to that friendship and to that quest.

Our own tradition is full of such people. As I grew up, there were people in my congregation whom my parents pointed to as saints, and they used that word. One of those persons was a maid; one was a CEO. The maid had never married. She first cared for her parents and then for other people. Her life exhibited joy as she served generously, and although never a biological mother, she attempted to be a mother to everyone. Her touch and glance gave me the sense that I was in touch with God. The other saint was the CEO of a small company. He gave so much money to the church that he was audited by the IRS for that reason. This made a great impression on my father, so the CEO entered the saint category at that point.

As a first-generation college student, I also have a real respect for another kind of education. As Joe Lapp has said, we have a relatively short history in higher education relative to other groups. But we have a long history of wisdom. Our emphasis on humility makes us eminently teachable. As Michael McPherson, president of Macalester College, said in his inaugural address: "Only the humble achieve excellence, since only the humble can learn." We can respect, and should respect, the wisdom in our tradition whether or not it has been blessed by formal education. We need to find ways to honour wisdom figures on our campuses. When we do, we are teaching an invisible curriculum.

Travel. There is also wisdom beyond our own tradition. Goshen College's international education program is important to the wisdom learning of students and their professors who go with them to far away places, to very different cultures, often to highly devout people. Whether or not they are Christians, the host families in foreign cultures have a wisdom tradition, and it is more visible to our students there than it might be at home. So they encounter elders in Africa or in Asia or in Central America in ways that draw out respect and these elders often strike them at an angle that they cannot be struck by at home. We need to find every way we can to encourage such encounters.

Our curriculum on campus can teach wisdom as well as travel abroad. We can give our students provocative things to read like this piece that a friend sent me through the Internet. It is called "The Invitation" and is attributed to Oriah Mountain Dreamer, Indian Elder.

> It doesn't interest me what you do for a living. I want to know what you ache for, and if you dare to dream of meeting your heart's longing. . . . It doesn't interest me to know where you live or how much money you have. I want to know if you can get up after a night of grief and despair, weary and bruised to the bone, and do what needs to be done for the children. It doesn't interest me who you know or how you came to be here. I want to know if you will stand in the center of the fire with me and not shrink back. It doesn't interest me where or what or with whom you have studied. I want to know what sustains you from the inside when all else falls away. I want to know if you can be alone with yourself and if you truly like the company you keep in the empty moments.

If we are going to have a curriculum, visible or invisible, that supports the development of those kinds of character traits, what will we have to do that we are not doing now? What will we have to become aware of in what we are already doing so that we can help others to know why we are doing it and how we can make it better?

Keep connected to nature. We need to make sure that our students do not lose contact with nature during their college experience. Several years ago, I took my students in an intensive literature course with me to The Hermitage in Michigan. The Hermitage is a nature retreat run by Gene and Mary Herr. We were studying the Romantic poets, so it was very appropriate to spend some time out in nature. Sometimes there were silences and students were allowed to roam on their own and reflect on what we had just read and spoken about. One of my students said to me, "Oh, if only I had known this place existed four years ago." Out of that comment, do you realize how noisy college campuses are and how easy it is for us to separate nature from what it is that we do? Many of our students crave the opportunity to be quiet--to sit near a tree and in front of the sky, reflecting. Experiences like these foster wisdom.

Celebrate the arts. Our campuses do celebrate the arts fairly well, but I think we can do even better, especially if we realize that the arts are part of the invisible curriculum that fosters wisdom traits in ourselves and our students. The arts combine students' social needs with their intellectual and spiritual needs in ways that aren't readily possible in the classroom.

At Goshen College the English department has several traditions that enhance the intellectual and spiritual climate of the campus. One of these is our Pinch Penny Press, started by Nick Lindsay, our poet in residence, over 20 years ago. We publish about five books every year that are written by students, faculty, and selected outsiders. These are real books made possible by advanced technology. Costs are so low that nearly all volumes pay for themselves in sales. When students publish a book, we have a reception and a public reading and all their friends come. This is a social event as well as something that stimulates the minds and spirits of the people who produce and buy and read the books.

Another similar tradition is Broadside publications. These are poems printed on card stock and signed by the poet: a student, faculty member, or campus guest. The one I brought with me is unusual because it is double-sided. The poems on both sides are about the life and death of a young Goshen College graduate named Alicia Showalter Reynolds. Some of you know her story because of stories carried by the Mennonite Press. She was a 1993 graduate of Goshen College, and she was my niece.

The story of Alicia's kidnapping as it unfolded over a six-month period of time when no one knew where she was, and then the discovery of her decomposed body, was the focus of life for our family and extended family, for the larger Mennonite community in Harrisonburg, Virginia, and for Alicia's friends and acquaintances throughout the church. Her story brought people together from many places. The two Broadside poems touch on some themes that have been important in this conference. Both use metaphors from nature in ways that show us the beauty of what could be called *Gelassenheit*, letting go, being the one consumed. They also reflect on the life of a student, 25 years old, who is an inspiration to me every day because I hope my own testimony to excellence in faith and work and relationship can be as strong as hers was at age 25.

Alicia left behind many traces of her faith. She graduated as a biology major from Goshen College and had a fellowship from Johns Hopkins University where she was studying schistosomiasis, a disease that kills millions of young children in Africa. She was working to find a cure for that disease when she was kidnapped and murdered.

I was in North Carolina on sabbatical leave last year and had very few close friends around me at the time, but I had made a new friend, Jane Tompkins, at Duke University. We had talked about many other things, and when this tragic event struck my life, she was a good listener. She wrote a poem to help me through grief and to pay tribute to a woman she had never met except through story. The poem is called "Her Wedding Ring." It mentions buzzards because the news reports of finding the body credited buzzards for alerting a viewer from afar to the presence of something that should be investigated. It turned out to be the body of Alicia. When her father, Harley Showalter, heard that story, he said, "Thank God for buzzards. Without them we would never know what had happened to Alicia."

Her Wedding Ring
for Shirley

High in the updraft
The buzzard sees her
Sees Alicia, the one
Who has made a perfect circle

Down in the bushes, far down
Among the weeds, she

Who studied microorganisms
So people in tropical places
Need not die
Too soon

Now, partially decomposed
Finishes her work.

Jane Tompkins

The second poem, on the other side of the Broadside, comes from Mary Linton, who is associate professor of biology at Goshen.

Women's Studies
for Alicia

When their young women's bodies
    splashed into the water,
I heard instead geese honking
    overhead,
the startled snort of a deer,
the sweet song of an ovenbird.

Last May
When they found you
Murdered and decaying
    in a Virginia forest,
The wildness went out of me.
I could no longer teach
    the ways of the coyote:
Loping through the fields
    on a nipping spring day,
    burrs and beggar-ticks in our fur
    and mice in our bellies.
No longer would we yip and yowl
    together under night skies,
sensing each other's starlit
    shadows.
I became domesticated,
A collie worrying after sheep.

Today
their pale golden bodies
    were dressed only in leaf-stained
    water and sunlight,
Sunlight that glinted from my

          wild yellow eyes
     as I turned by tail to the barn
     and trotted for the woods.

Mary Linton

The arts have power to heal terrible wounds. They can teach us deep lessons for present and future application.

Sciences. The great gift the sciences bring to wisdom teaching is the gift of attention. The philosopher Simone Weil, in her book *Waiting for God*, has written eloquently about the importance of disciplining our minds to see and think. She sees school studies having theological meaning because they can train us to be ready when God has something strong and powerful to teach us. Although science is famous for secular and even anti-religious thought, it can be the cradle of faith and wisdom also. The "new science," especially in the field of physics, is teaching us mystery and awe again. These are wisdom's handmaidens.

Sports. It may seem odd to place sports in the category of powerful practices for teaching wisdom, but consider these possibilities. If science stretches our attention span and our minds, athletics stretch our bodies and our relationships. An education that diminishes the body diminishes the wholeness that permeates wisdom literature and is contained in every living thing. Exercising is necessary for health, and fitness of body teaches us what wholeness feels like physically. The exertion it takes to be fit in body is not different in form from the exertion it takes to stay close to God and to stay close to a scientific or artistic puzzle.

Our institutions should encourage all students to participate in sports and not just focus on the gladiatorial skills of a few. If we do not help students to feel at home in their bodies, we have lost a powerful opportunity.

Technology. Here's an even more surprising addition to a list of powerful practices. How can technology teach wisdom? It can't. It can only be a tool, but if we have wisdom on our campuses—and we want to connect with wisdom elsewhere in the church and the world—we are living in an exciting age. I do not know how the world-wide Mennonite Church and our colleges in North America will connect, but today we have new opportunities and tomorrow we will have even more. My predecessor in office, Hank Weaver, interim Goshen College president, July 1-December 31, 1996, dreams of a Mennonite World University. Perhaps there will be one some day.

Music. I spoke of the need to celebrate the arts earlier, but I believe music plays a special wisdom role on our campuses. It is a portable art form and it can be practiced collectively. Therefore, it is an especially powerful practice for a people whose ancestors went to their martyrdom so full of music—praise to God—that their persecutors had to screw their tongues to the roof of their mouths. The *Ausbund* and the many hymn books that followed contain the irrepressible joy of living life so fully and freely that one is prepared at all times to die. But we have experienced even more wisdom in our music. When we sing, we conspire, we literally breath with each other. We tune our voices to each other and by doing so, we feel, in both body and spirit, the truth that the sum is greater than the parts. We touch God's spirit as we touch each other's.

Integrated residence life and academic life. On all of our campuses, we strive for, and often succeed in creating, an education that refuses to separate the secular and the sacred, living and learning. The saints among us have shown the way. Today we have great challenges in this area because our students have many anti-wisdom influences in their lives. We have to challenge these. The standards we attempt to establish with regard to sexuality, drinking, smoking and drugs, for example, should not be rules we impose in order not to disturb the neighbours or the constituency. They should be understood by faculty and students as part of our curriculum—the invisible part—that builds high character and not just high grades. We need to engage faculty and staff—not just student life personnel—in conversation and in leading by example so that students can see such things as: a) the benefits of chastity and fidelity; b) the benefits of having fun without taking the risk of overindulgence in alcohol or other potentially harmful substances; c) what a person on a spiritual quest looks like, sounds like, talks like, listens like.

Conclusion   The people needed for this idealistic enterprise, brothers and sisters, are the people in this room and the many others on our campuses who will give themselves to this high calling. We need to be each other's bread and wine tonight and in the millennium to come. We need to remember William Wordsworth's words from The Prelude: "What we have loved, others will love/and we will teach them how."

Let us conclude by conspiring in song. I have asked Shirley King, professor of music at Bethel College, to lead us in the 9th century Latin hymn "Ubi Caritas." As she does so, let us all allow ourselves the deep pleasure of recommitting ourselves to the Wisdom way.

----

11 On Being a Mennonite Professor

Shirley Sprunger King[1]

Introduction As I pondered my assignment, "To reflect on being a Mennonite professor," I wondered how I would be different, or see my role as a professor differently in a non-Mennonite institution. I realized very quickly that my varied experiences in Mennonite higher education give me a unique perspective. Certainly these experiences have moulded my understanding of my role at Bethel College. I'm a graduate of Bluffton—my whole family went there—my parents and several uncles and aunts plus all of my siblings went and graduated from there. My husband and oldest son and daughter-in-law are Goshen graduates, my second son a junior at Bethel. I've taught at Hesston, Tabor and Bethel and enjoyed a wonderful sabbatical semester at AMBS two years ago. And through it all I have a special appreciation of the different personalities each of these institutions has. (And maybe I feel a bit more schizophrenic than most of you here.)

I remember waltzing into my first organ lesson as a sophomore at Bluffton College and announcing to the organ teacher, that I was going to be "an organ major." Before the end of that year my real dream was to be a professor, an organ professor in a college—hopefully a Mennonite one.

Some 13 years later, after graduate school, marriage and MCC, I arrived at Bethel College as the "new organ instructor" in a 1/8th position, hired virtually sight-unseen by Marion Deckert, then academic dean at Bethel. These 20 years at Bethel College have been good ones, certainly challenging and enriching, in the best sense. And along the way I have been aware of the role of key professors in my life—my

---

[1]Associate Professor of Music, Bethel College.

mentors--those who were often there to help me sort out the important issues in my college years and dream dreams for my future. During those years, three people in particular were very influential in my educational quest.

Role Models As a freshman in college, I had the good fortune to enroll in Robert Kreider's "Contemporary Africa" class where I learned about colonial governments in Africa, the land where I'd grown up. I still remember reading Alan Paton's *Cry the Beloved Country* and encountering Dr. Kreider's probing questions and affirmations on my book report. Through his gentle prodding and obvious interest in helping me ask some difficult questions about my assumptions, I learned the importance of seeking truth and understanding in complex political and social situations. When we moved to Newton 14 years later, I thanked him for opening up a totally new world in Africa for me. His response was the characteristic question of a historian. "What year did you take that class?" he asked. After hearing my response, he apologized profusely saying that that was the first year he'd taught the Africa class and had made so many improvements during the following years, he was sorry I had taken it then. I assured him the course had been very important in my thinking and reconsidered world view.

The second individual was Doris Lora, the intellectual and refined organ teacher I valued so much in my early study. She modeled for me an intelligent young woman on the Bluffton music faculty. I remember her standards to be very high and yet she found ways to keep the challenges within my reach. She taught me the value and rewards of disciplined practice, and for her patience and encouragement I am very grateful.

From James Bixel I learned to dream dreams for a future in the music profession. Mr. B., as he was warmly known to the music majors, knew better than anyone I've yet met, how to ask questions—whether it was in music theory, in the fine arts course where I served as his assistant, or meaning in life. His genuine concern for and interest in his students was unparalleled in my college experience. He modeled the inquiring mind at its highest level and believed in educating "seekers." Mr. B. had an incredible passion for Mozart. Through his eyes Mozart came alive for me and to this day I do not hear the music of Mozart without thinking of James Bixel. Indeed, as I consider what it means to be a mentor these days, I remember with real appreciation the hours Mr. Bixel and I spent discussing theology, career and spiritual concerns, and many deeply personal issues. Few individuals have been more important to my philosophical and spiritual development than James Bixel. For his unwavering belief in me and continuing interest over the years, I am forever indebted.

I acknowledge the positive and important influence of teachers like Doris Lora, but perhaps even more crucial for me has been the sustained encouragement of men like James Bixel who have helped young women like me strive to be all we can be. These are but three models of which I am conscious, and I believe models that are worthy of emulation.

Being a Teacher As I ponder my role in the academic world, particularly my role in a Mennonite college, I realize that there are three important aspects: *first* to teach an academic discipline; *second*, to share my personal faith narrative; and *third*, to demonstrate how each shapes the other. In conjunction with these I would add a deep concern for educating the whole individual and building meaningful relationships with students and colleagues. I've learned that these relationships are developed primarily outside of the classroom in many different ways.

Teaching an academic discipline. The choice of what academic subject to teach has been relatively easy for me. I knew when I entered college that I would study and major in music. Although I had interests in several other areas, music was clearly my strongest suit and my passion for it went back to my third grade days when I started piano lessons and my mother never had to tell me to practice. In fact, how I've wished over the years that my sons might have inherited just a portion of that passion I have for music. There are also times I long to see just a glimpse of discipline or passion for music in some of my students. But alas . . .

At Bethel we talk about opening up our minds and our hearts to the world around us. We believe the classroom is an open door--a place for examining the tough questions of living in this place at this time. Critical thinking, so crucial to the intellectual pursuit, provides a framework for interpreting the knowledge gained on our campuses. Just as I can remember with deep appreciation the faithful listening and counter questions of my mentors, I find some of my most rewarding hours spent not teaching the basics of music theory or organ performance, but rather helping students learn to ask important questions, questions that matter in the larger scheme. Don't get me wrong. I'm not skipping over the fundamental basics in music, but I find a special delight in the opportunity to ask unexpected questions about the music we are studying, and why some of these questions must really be important to us as students of music.

I love teaching music and I can't imagine a life without it! We often hear that music is the universal language! I continue to ponder whether that platitude has validity or if it is just a wonderful sentimental concept we musicians like to hold. This idea of universality might touch on the outer edges of the concept of "world view" in the discipline of music something that I particularly value coming out of my own experiences.

On the first day in my "Introduction to Music" class, I use an exercise that requires critical listening to four very different types of music and then I ask the students to suggest adjectives that describe what they think the music is communicating. Based on my findings over the semesters, there are some sounds/music with universal qualities that produce striking similarities in labelling emotions and responses. And, these bridge different cultures. The primary purpose of my course is to create perceptive listeners of a wide range of musical styles, this gained through required listening and designated concerts on campus. For most students today, music is understood only as entertainment. (I suspect because most students have some experience with music, if only turning on MTV, they believe my course to be the most accessible and perhaps the easiest of the three options they have in the fine arts.) As you might guess, there are many students who have never heard an opera or orchestra, who are, in fact, *very* sure that they would never be able to appreciate, much less understand these types of music. The content of the course is roughly half classical, the other half popular, jazz, etc. hoping to find some common denominators on which to build.

One of the most important aspects of this introductory course is introducing the non-western musics (or world music) to my North American students. And the highlight of the semester for me (and I believe my class) is the involvement of the international students in the course. With few exceptions, these students from Japan, India, Spain, and this past semester Guatemala and Nepal, have been able to share their music with my class and bring real life and energy to music from the distant land. Their contributions have proved essential in creating a broader understanding of how music contributes to a society, and has provided a wonderful foundation for the rest of the class to examine how music functions in our society. The discipline of "Ethnomusic-ology" is relatively new in the academic world, but is an important part of my understanding of a broad introduction to music in today's world and fits in well in the liberal arts curriculum.

In addition to promoting a broader world view of music, I find a special delight in sharing the video on John Cage, "I have nothing to say, and I'm saying it." It is amazing how, after seeing that video, students hear sounds around them differently and can be engaged in some incredible discussions. (These years later, I still vividly remember James Bixel's fascination with John Cage's work in the 1960s.)

Most of us come to the teaching profession with a strong orientation and background in a specific field of study. Perhaps one of the most difficult aspects of teaching in a small private college is the need to be flexible and to teach courses that aren't in our specialty. The ability to feel some level of comfort in teaching content outside of a chosen area is crucial to success for most of us in Mennonite higher education. I've especially admired colleagues who seem to do this with ease! I often come away from these experiences feeling more like a "jack of too many trades and master of none."

When I attend professional conferences, such as the American Guild of Organists, as I will again next week in Wisconsin, the first day or so I find myself being somewhat envious of my colleagues in large music programs who teach organ literature, give private organ lessons, have scheduled time to practice, and find themselves on a concert circuit. What a great position, I think quietly. No obligation to learn how to use the most up-to-date computer music software to teach aural skills in music theory. But, before the second day is over, I realize again why I love my position in a liberal arts college so much. The opportunities in the faculty lounge and lunch tables to interact with my colleagues in the sciences and humanities is something I no longer take for granted. The richness of these experiences and the awareness of what I gain from them, help me understand why teaching in a school like Bethel is so important for my own growth as a scholar, professional, and human being.

I don't have time to go into some other aspects of teaching music in a church-related college. But I at least want to acknowledge the tension that inevitably exists finding a balance between the academic expectations and needs of a music curriculum, and filling the PR and church relations arm of the college. Here I would offer that among other aspects, we can be (and need to be) more intentional in helping to stretch our constituents' experience through music—not choosing to perform only the easy listening and most quickly appreciated.

Sharing my personal faith narrative. The process of sharing my personal faith journey brings different challenges to my life as a professor on the Bethel campus. No doubt I am still reacting to my background as a missionary kid. Although I grew up with and know the evangelical language, I have never been comfortable with it and I find myself looking for different words that, for me, are more authentic ways to express my faith.

I teach my students that there is no music that is in itself inherently sacred or secular—rather, it is the context and function that determines our understanding of the sacred and secular in music. Within these discussions about music I often find opportunities to share experiences of when I have encountered God. Two masterpieces that I teach regularly in Music History, Bach's *Passion According to St. Matthew* and Benjamin Britten's *War Requiem*, provide unlimited opportunities to discuss philosophical and theological elements that are critical to the broader understanding of these works. It is impossible to study the way Bach musically portrays Matthew's text without experiencing anew the story of Christ's trial, crucifixion, and death. Indeed, Bach's depth of faith comes through loud and clear in his music, in such things as the musical tone painting setting the text of Peter's denial and weeping. I invite anyone who has not been moved by this short but powerful recitative, to listen again with late 20th-century ears and realize that Bach is not only setting this Gospel story, but helping us experience today the pity of our selfish and self-centred world.

Important elements like these often become part of a broader discussion including, for the Britten *War Requiem*, whether there are responsibilities of artists to be prophetic in response to world issues and events. The juxtaposing of Wilfred Owens' poetry, written before he was killed in the First World War, with the ancient Latin text of the Mass, bring new meaning to the words, "Lord, have mercy on us."

Likewise, it is impossible to talk theoretically about the harsh and ugly sounds of the 48 string instruments in Penderecki's *Threnody for the Victims of Hiroshima* without identifying the underlying violence and impact of war in our world. What, I ask, is the artist's role or responsibility in society? Is it merely to record events and ideas in a musical setting? Or is there also a responsibility to be prophetic and warn about the terrors of war and the violence of hatred and racism? Someday I hope for the opportunity to teach a course that looks exclusively at compositions that have been written not as pure music, but seem to be prophetic and have a social and spiritual message to share with all who will listen.

How do academics and personal faith interrelate The demonstration of how the academic discipline and a personal faith narrative shape each other is not so easily identified or measured. I know that there have been many musical experiences that have strengthened my faith in God, and have literally been "awesome" encounters with the Almighty. Perhaps it is primarily in the modelling that integration of faith and discipline are best communicated in the academic community. In the best sense, this is the teaching that is done in and out of the classroom. Whether it is on field trips or in social gatherings on campus or in homes, students observe the actions of professors. As a student, I remember paying close attention to the way my mentors integrated their academic and professional knowledge with the activities in their personal and social lives. I remember my appreciation of hearing what motivated my mentors in their career choices and how the spiritual elements of their daily lives were critical in the decisions they made. Years later I enjoy sharing how my education on a Mennonite college campus has helped shape some of my career choices as well. The eight years I spent with MCC have given me a concern for service and especially for understanding peoples of other cultures and ethnic backgrounds. These values certainly come through when I have opportunities to share my knowledge and appreciation for music from around the world. Some of this music has little connection with traditional spirituality, at least in the way we understand it in the Western world. But I continue to look for authentic ways to share how this unfamiliar music is every bit a part of God's kingdom and amazing creation as are the musical masterpieces we associate with the Christian worship experience.

Students pick up very quickly our expressed respect for values of the educational and spiritual mission on our campuses. Our behaviour and attitudes toward students, shown through our caring and concern about their lives, in and out of the classroom, are significant indicators of our real interest in and commitment to relating to students in our community of learners. One of the most important characteristics I remember experiencing in my relationships with my teachers is their "faithful listening." Yet, how difficult it seems some days to listen to students who only finds negative things to say about their experiences in the academic environment. And how easy it is to lose the opportunity to hear what these students really wanted to say, but weren't sure they could trust me with the most important thing happening to them at that time in their life.

These really meaningful relationships can only happen when we are willing to take the risk of being vulnerable. Numerous examples come to mind of how students have come looking for a listening ear that communicates a sense of compassion. No doubt because I once needed those same kinds of ears, I have a special empathy for these seekers.

Perhaps the most difficult aspect of mentoring relationships is the fine line and balancing act we must play in the unequal roles we have with students. The potential for misunderstanding in maintaining academic rigour in the relationship with a student who is less gifted increases and produces a different kind of vulnerability in the mentor-mentee alliance. Yet these students often are precisely the ones who need the most attention and encouragement.

Educational wholeness means for me the linking of beliefs, values and academic disciplines in the quest for truly educated individuals. The concept of educational wholeness is not new. Indeed, we talk of educating the whole person and believe that this is one of the most important aspects or characteristics of our students' education on our campus.

As I look back to the fall of 1977, one of the first hard questions that awaited me as a first year organ teacher at Bethel came from a thoughtful senior organ and Bible and Religion major. He wondered, after spending eight years with MCC—the last three in Haiti—how I could seriously consider the enormous expense of either repairing or replacing the large organ literally dying in Bethel's chapel.

What part of this decision is aesthetics and what part stewardship, I wondered? And how do they intersect in this instance? In the arts, these questions often become even more difficult to address in the Mennonite constituency because of our heritage of simplicity and the concept of the arts as being nice, but generally unnecessary. Grappling with these types of issues must continue to be part of the academic inquiry in a Mennonite institution.

As I addressed the question of what to do with the organ, at least part of the discussion had to do with the question of what role organ instruction had in our curriculum. Years later before embarking on my doctorate in organ performance, I pondered why I was teaching organ in the first place. Was it only my personal passion or might there be some special merit in a Mennonite college with a strong music tradition?

Organ departments in large universities around the country were closing, due to the small student enrollment. That wasn't our problem. But when I looked at why a Mennonite college might find this instruction worthwhile (besides the historical facts that organ was part of the early college curriculum at Bethel), I acknowledged that my primary purpose was to introduce my students to important literature for the organ and to prepare them, as far as is possible, to be competent church musicians. Another part of the discussion involved the role of the organ in Bethel's chapel. In the past years I have known students who have been inspired by the fine quality of the new instrument to study the organ, because, as one student told me, "I've never heard an organ sound like this before." I continue to cherish the opportunities I regularly have to share my passion for music in the church, especially quality congregational singing and we work at modelling that regularly in our weekly chapel services.

In addition to sharing my concern for quality instrumental music in the college and church with my students, I believe that by virtue of my position in the academic community, I have an obligation to nurture my role and relationship with the broader Mennonite constituency. I believe that there must be a continuing dialogue between the college and the church on many topics, including music in the church. And it seems natural to me that the academic community has a responsibility for providing resources for the continuing education of our church musicians. In our tradition, music, more than the other arts, is a vital part of worship and I believe the colleges must be actively involved in the ongoing discussion about how we use music to enhance our worship experiences. The potential tensions and challenges in this relationship between college and church are important and necessary, and I truly believe our discussions can be constructive when we build on foundations of integrity and authenticity. (I have had some very gratifying experiences working in consulting roles in several churches.)

We often talk about being a community of seekers and learners. Over the years I've been intrigued with who my community is and the many places where I find my community. In addition to the expected—my colleagues in the academic enterprise—I find a stimulating and growing sense of community with my students. During the past 20 months I have had the privilege and awesome task of serving on Bethel's strategic planning task force. I've learned much about Bethel—about her strengths and her weaknesses. When it came time to form sub-committees to focus on specific issues the task force had identified, I hoped I might be named to something concrete—perhaps facilities—something you can tell is getting done or not! Instead, in many ways I got my biggest nightmare and was asked to chair the committee studying ways to improve our residence life. But it wasn't a nightmare for long.

From the onset it was clear that there were numerous issues that we needed to address. I spent January mostly in meetings—focus groups to look at tissues of substance abuse, issues of the academic environment on campus, community-building tasks that help us to work together within the diversity of our campus community, and at the spiritual dimensions of our lives on the Bethel campus. As complex and troubling as some of the issues were, I was encouraged by the active involvement of students and their ideas and suggestions. The discussions reaffirmed for me the type of students we have at Bethel—students who are thoughtful and concerned about the quality of life on our campus and not just the academic exercises of being a student. I was impressed with the depth of conversation we had on numerous occasions. I continue to be concerned about the ways we, in the academic community, encourage each other to ask important and difficult questions, but don't always make sure we are still around to struggle together with the tough answers we sometimes find. I'm convinced that there must be a balance between the intellectual rigour and the caring and supportive community of individuals searching for a meaningful faith within common values and goals on our campuses. I'd like to think this is what sets us apart from the mainstream of liberal art colleges. I found it particularly rewarding to find students and faculty who are committed to working hard on these and other important issues that affect the quality of our lives in the academic community. And for me, this was a major community-building experience. (Oh, incidently, hours before jumping on the plane for this conference, I received an invitation to be on a facilities task force, for the remodelling of Goering Hall, the men's residence hall. I'll learn not to wish so hard in the future.)

One of the other highlights for me as a member of the Bethel community is the privilege of being a faculty examiner for the oral portion of our senior-level religion course, Basic Issues of Faith and Life. I have been thankful for the opportunities to witness, first hand, how some students have grappled with difficult questions of faith and learning. It has been rewarding to interact with students who have been able to see how the intellectual learning in their disciplines can be related to their faith, and how their faith informs what is important about the challenges they will face out in the "real world."

I remember a particular session with an African-American student who brought new vision and insights to Toni Morrison's book, *Beloved*, based on his experience in the Black community. The discussion that ensued with the white student was truly a gift to all five of us in the room, and one for which I am very grateful. The growth I have witnessed from seeing many of these students who I knew first as freshmen in my introductory music class has often been extraordinary. When I witness their ability to integrate a wide variety of knowledge with ethical issues, I remember again why I teach at Bethel. I suspect this is one of the most important aspects of the liberal education or educating for wholeness in the students' academic experience on our campus. I can truly say these have been some of my most rewarding hours.

The integrative life of education requires more work than is often perceived at first. As faculty, our real responsibilities lie in nurturing and educating our students for a life of significance in this world. Beyond excellence in the classroom, we must work at modelling honesty, integrity and discipline for our students.

I share many of Ted's concerns (see *supra* chapter 8) about how faculty relate to administrators. I'm sure the administrative roles would be much easier to deal with without faculty cynicism and stubbornness. Somehow, I doubt that Bethel has the corner on these! The emotional energy of working together sometimes seems very costly, but I think it is crucial to our common understanding of our mission. One idea and interest I have had for some years now is a faculty exchange program within our institutions. I know how I have been enriched by the cross-fertilization I've experienced being a part of other Mennonite institutions. Might this be a program and part of our integration process?

Conclusion For our last chapel at Bethel this spring, I was invited to reflect and share what I was thankful for this year. I remember being thankful for a good year—so much better than the one before it—and thankful for opportunities to be part of a campus that is working to build a stronger community. And, as I considered the larger and long-term picture, I found myself being especially thankful for the opportunity to teach in and be apart of Bethel College.

When I hear from alumni how Bethel made a difference in their lives—how the relationships they developed at Bethel continue to be important, how they appreciated the opportunities they had to develop both their intellectual capacities and grow in their spiritual lives, how they learned to ask hard questions about their faith (or lack of it) and not be afraid that the world would cave in on them—I am truly thankful for Bethel College.

These past days have truly been inspiring. I have wished more faculty from our institutions could have been here. I continue to appreciate the tradition of Mennonite higher education, both as a product of it and for the opportunities to be a part of the current enterprise. I believe that we have much to offer our young people and each other, and that we must continue to search for meaningful ways to make a difference in the education we offer. Indeed, we must be there sharing and encouraging our students as they dream for our future together.
